剑桥美国小说新论 · 3

New Essays on

Go Tell it on the Mountain

《向苍天呼吁》新论

Trudier Harris 编

著作权合同登记　图字：01-2006-7205 号
图书在版编目（CIP）数据

《向苍天呼吁》新论 = New Essays on *Go Tell It on the Mountain* / 哈里斯（Harris，T.）编．—北京：北京大学出版社，2007.1
（剑桥美国小说新论·3）

ISBN 978-7-301-11385-1

Ⅰ．向…　Ⅱ．哈…　Ⅲ．长篇小说-文学研究-美国-现代-英文
Ⅳ．I712.074

中国版本图书馆 CIP 数据核字（2006）第 152256 号

Originally published by Cambridge University Press in 1996

This reprint edition is published with the permission of the Syndicate of the Press of the University of Cambridge, Cambridge, England.

书　　名：New Essays on *Go Tell It on the Mountain*
　　　　　《向苍天呼吁》新论
著作责任者：Trudier Harris　编
组稿编辑：张　冰
责任编辑：刘　强
标准书号：ISBN 978-7-301-11385-1/I·0856
出版发行：北京大学出版社
地　　址：北京市海淀区成府路 205 号　100871
网　　址：http://www.pup.cn
电　　话：邮购部 62752015　发行部 62750672
　　　　　编辑部 62767347　出版部 62754962
电子邮箱：zbing@pup.pku.edu.cn
印 刷 者：三河市新世纪印务有限公司
经 销 者：新华书店
　　　　　650 毫米×980 毫米　16 开本　10.75 印张　176 千字
　　　　　2007 年 1 月第 1 版　2007 年 12 月第 2 次印刷
定　　价：20.00 元

导　读

北京大学英语系教授　陶洁

近年来，美国文学在我国很受欢迎。大专院校英语系纷纷开设美国文学选读和专题课，学生从中学到的大部分内容是美国小说。不仅如此，在本科毕业论文、硕士论文或博士论文方面，学生所选题材也大多为关于某部美国小说或某个美国小说家。然而，我们的学生往往热衷理论而对作品或作家缺乏深入细致的了解和分析。他们往往先大谈理论规则，然后罗列一些例证，不能很好地把理论和文本融会贯通，恰如其分地结合在一起。在这种情况下，我们需要一些好的参考资料来帮助学生更好地认识和理解他们在阅读或研究的作品和作家。《剑桥美国小说新论》正是这样一套优秀的参考书。

这套丛书的负责人是曾经主编过《哥伦比亚美国文学史》的艾默里·埃利奥特教授，并且由英国剑桥大学出版社在上世纪80年代中期开始陆续出书，至今仍在发行并出版新书，目前已有五十多种，不仅出平装本还有精装本。一套书发行二十多年还有生命力，估计还会继续发行，主要因为它确实从学生的需要出发，深受他们和教师的喜爱。

《剑桥美国小说新论》的编排方式比较统一。根据主编制定的原则，每本书针对一部美国文学历史上有名望的大作家的一本经典小说，论述者都是研究这位作家的知名学者。开篇是一位权威专家的论述，主要论及作品的创作过程、出版历史、当年的评价以及小说发表以来不同时期的主要评论和阅读倾向。随后是四到五篇论述，从不同角度用不同的批评方法对作品进行分析和阐释。这些文章并非信手拈来，而是专门为这套丛书撰写的，运用的理论都比较新，其中不乏颇有新意的真知灼见。书的最后是为学生进一步学习和研究而提供的参考书目。由此可见，编书的学者们为了帮助学生确实煞费苦心，努力做到尽善尽美。

这五十多种书有早期美国文学家库珀的《最后的莫希干人》，也有当代试验小说大师品钦的《拍卖第49号》和厄普代克那曾被《时代》杂志评为1923年以来100部最佳小说之一的《兔子，跑吧!》；有我们比较熟悉的麦尔维尔的《白鲸》，也有我们还不太了解的他的《漂亮水手》；有中国学生很喜欢的海明威的长篇小说《永别了，武器》，令人想不到的是还有一本论述他所有的短篇小说的集子。有些大作家如亨利·詹姆斯、威廉·福克纳等都有两三本作品入选，但它们都分别有专门的集子。丛书当然涉及已有定论的大作家，包括黑人和白人作家（可惜还没有华裔作家的作品），但也包括20世纪70年代妇女运动中发掘出来的如凯特·肖邦的《觉醒》和佐拉·尼尔·赫斯顿的《他们眼望上苍》，甚至还有我国读者很熟悉的斯托夫人的《汤姆叔叔的小屋》。当年这部小说曾经风靡美国，在全世界都有一定的影响，后来被贬为“政治宣传”作品，从此在美国文学史上销声匿迹。70年代后随着要求扩大文学经典中女性和少数族裔作家的呼声日益高涨，人们才开始重新评价这部作品，分析它对日后妇女作家的影响、对黑人形象的塑造，甚至它在美国文学的哥特式传统中的地位等等。

这样的例子还有很多，例如威廉·迪恩·豪威尔斯和他的《赛拉斯·拉帕姆的发迹》。以前人们只肯定他在发展现实主义文学和理论方面的贡献，对他的作品除了《赛拉斯·拉帕姆的发迹》评价都不太高。但在这本新论文集子里编者对已有定论进行挑战，强调豪威尔斯的小说、他的现实主义跟当时的社会经济文化现状有很大的关系。他的小说既有其文学形式，又是一种社会力量。另外一位19世纪新英格兰作家萨拉·奥尼·裘威特过去一向被看成是乡土作家，现在学者们用女性主义观点强调她的《尖枞树之乡》对美国文学的贡献，分析当年的种族、民族主义和文学市场对她写作的影响。用封底宣传语言来说，这本集子对美国文学研究、女性主义批评理论和美国研究等方面都会引起很大的兴趣。

还有一本书似乎在我们国家很少有人提起过——亨利·罗思的《就说是睡着了》。此书在20世纪30年代曾经风靡一时，此后长期销声匿迹，60年代又再度受到推崇。现在这部小说则是上面提到的《时代》杂志100部优秀小说中的一部，被认为是上个世纪头50年里最为出色的美国犹太小说、最优秀的现代主义小说之一。评论家认为集子里的文章采用心理分析、社会历史主义等批评方法探讨了有关移民、族裔和文化归属等多方面的问题。

这套集子里还出现了令人信服的新论点。很长时间内海明威一直被认为是讨厌女人的大男子主义者。但在关于他的短篇小说的论述里，作者通过分析《在密执安北部》，令人信服地证明海明威其实对妇女充满同情。不仅如此，这一论断还瓦解了海明威在《太阳照样升起》中充分暴露他的厌女症的定论。

然而，作者们并不侈谈理论或玩弄理论名词，所有的论断都是既以一定的理论为基础，又对文本进行深入的分析；既把理论阐述得深入浅出，又把作品分析得丝丝入扣，让人不由得不信服。他们能够做到这一点完全是因为他们了解学生的水平和需要。

我认为《剑桥美国小说新论》是一套很好的参考书。北京大学出版社购买版权，出版这套书是个有益于外国文学研究教学的决定。

Contents

Series Editor's Preface

In literary criticism the last twenty-five years have been particularly fruitful. Since the rise of the New Criticism in the 1950s, which focused attention of critics and readers upon the text itself – apart from history, biography, and society – there has emerged a wide variety of critical methods which have brought to literary works a rich diversity of perspectives: social, historical, political, psychological, economic, ideological, and philosophical. While attention to the text itself, as taught by the New Critics, remains at the core of contemporary interpretation, the widely shared assumption that works of art generate many different kinds of interpretations has opened up possibilities for new readings and new meanings.

Before this critical revolution, many works of American literature had come to be taken for granted by earlier generations of readers as having an established set of recognized interpretations. There was a sense among many students that the canon was established and that the larger thematic and interpretative issues had been decided. The task of the new reader was to examine the ways in which elements such as structure, style, and imagery contributed to each novel's acknowledged purpose. But recent criticism has brought these old assumptions into question and has thereby generated a wide variety of original, and often quite surprising, interpretations of the classics, as well as of rediscovered works such as Kate Chopin's *The Awakening*, which has only recently entered the canon of works that scholars and critics study and that teachers assign their students.

The aim of The American Novel Series is to provide students of American literature and culture with introductory critical

guides to American novels and other important texts now widely read and studied. Usually devoted to a single work, each volume begins with an introduction by the volume editor, a distinguished authority on the text. The introduction presents details of the work's composition, publication history, and contemporary reception, as well as a survey of the major critical trends and readings from first publication to the present. This overview is followed by four or five original essays, specifically commissioned from senior scholars of established reputation and from outstanding younger critics. Each essay presents a distinct point of view, and together they constitute a forum of interpretative methods and of the best contemporary ideas on each text.

It is our hope that these volumes will convey the vitality of current critical work in American literature, generate new insights and excitement for students of American literature, and inspire new respect for and new perspectives upon these major literary texts.

Emory Elliott
University of California, Riverside

1

Introduction

TRUDIER HARRIS

Background and Composition

Go Tell It on the Mountain, James Baldwin's first novel, was published in 1953. It had a long and extensive history of composition, extending across two continents and at least three countries. Baldwin had conceived the idea for the novel in the early 1940s, when he was about seventeen. He would write and rewrite it over the next ten years. An autobiographical composition, the novel takes its subject matter from the troubled relationship between Baldwin and his stepfather, David Baldwin. Little Jimmy was almost three years old in 1927 when his mother, Emma Burdis Jones, married David Baldwin, who legitimized his existence by adopting him. But the legal embrace did not mirror an emotional embrace. A history of racism and religion informed David's interactions with his adopted stepson. The elder Baldwin had come to Harlem from Louisiana, where he had been a preacher. Having less status, but being no less devout in Harlem, he held his family to strict interpretations of biblical texts. Wives were to be obedient and children were to be helpful but invisible; neither was to challenge the authority of the father who, following biblical injunction, was head of his household.

David Baldwin frequently took out his frustrations on the young Jimmy. He considered his stepson ugly and remarked that James had the mark of the devil on him. James's successes at school, which earned him the approval and applause of his white teachers, only exacerbated David. When James was "nine or ten," he wrote a play that was directed by one of his white schoolteachers. Her interest in him inspired her to approach his father about James attending a "real" play. Although theatergoing was forbidden in the Baldwin house, James watched his father capitulate to the white teacher and grant permission for him to accompany her to the theater. His father had questioned her motives before her arrival, and it was only his general fear of whites that prompted him to give very reluctant consent to the outing. In spite of this woman's help when David Baldwin was laid off from work, he never trusted her and warned James that his "white friends in high places were not really" his friends and that he would see when he grew older "how white people would do anything to keep a Negro down. Some of them could be nice, he admitted, but none of them were to be trusted and most of them were not even nice. The best thing was to have as little to do with them as possible."[1] This attitude echoes almost precisely the opinion of Gabriel Grimes in *Go Tell It on the Mountain*. Baldwin recounts from the point of view of John, Gabriel's stepson:

> His father said that all white people were wicked, and that God was going to bring them low. He said that white people were never to be trusted, and that they told nothing but lies, and that not one of them had ever loved a nigger. He, John, was a nigger, and he would find out, as soon as he got a little older, how evil white people could be.[2]

David Baldwin could not accept a world in which whites were anything but mean and hateful to blacks. His inability to change his attitudes with his change of geography, combined with his treatment of James, led to an intense hatred that the stepson would nurture for the stepfather. Baldwin's composition of *Go Tell It on the Mountain* was in many ways an extended rite of exorcism. He was trying in part to rid himself of the demons of hatred his stepfather had instilled in him. "I had to understand the forces, the experience, the life that shaped him," Baldwin would later comment, "before I could grow up myself, before I could become a writer. . . . I became a writer by tearing that book up for ten years."[3]

Baldwin recalls the strained relationship between him and his father in the title essay in *Notes of a Native Son* (1955). In that essay, Baldwin reviews his father's life, his behavior toward his wife and children, and the overwhelming bitterness that consumed him:

> He could be chilling in the pulpit and indescribably cruel in his personal life and he was certainly the most bitter man I have ever met. . . . When he took one of his children on his knee to play, the child always became fretful and began to cry; when he tried to help one of us with our homework the absolutely unabating tension which emanated from him caused our minds and our tongues to become paralyzed, so that he, scarcely knowing why, flew into a rage and the child, not knowing why, was punished. If it ever entered his head to bring a surprise home for his children, it was, almost unfailingly, the wrong surprise and even the big watermelons he often brought home on his back in the summertime led to the most appalling scenes. I do not remember, in all those years, that one of his children was ever glad to see him come home.[4]

His father, Baldwin asserted, "had lived and died in an intolerable bitterness of spirit."[5] Baldwin wondered, on his father's death in 1943, if that bitterness had not now become his own heritage. He had to find a way of reconciling bitter memories and hatred with the need to move forward into a healthy and hate-free future.

During his father's lifetime, however, Baldwin was never able to overcome his negative feelings toward him. Angered perhaps that his father was perennially impregnating his mother, and providing yet another baby for whom the young Jimmy, being the eldest child, had to assume caretaking responsibilities, Baldwin's hatred of his father intensified with the years. Baldwin escaped as soon as he was physically – if not financially – able. With his move first to New Jersey when he was seventeen and shortly thereafter to Greenwich Village, he separated himself from his father physically, but not psychologically. Troubled father/son relationships would prove to be a recurring theme in Baldwin's works. He later attempted to provide a literary healing in *If Beale Street Could Talk* (1974), in which a father's love for his son is so sincere that his inability to get the son out of jail leads him to commit suicide.

Equally central to the composition of *Go Tell It on the Mountain* is Baldwin's religious experience. In "Down at the Cross: Letter from a Region in My Mind," the second of the two essays in *The Fire Next Time* (1963), Baldwin discusses the physical and spiritual threats he began to feel at the age of fourteen. His own awakening to sexual desire was matched by the attempts of persons in his neighborhood to use him sexually, thus forcing a heightened awareness of the potential to sin and to be damned eternally for it. An acute sense of vulnerability to the forces around him – girls who were taught to begin looking for husbands, adults who exploited children sexually, cops who beat up little black boys – brought young Jimmy to the realization that not only his body but his soul was endangered. As early as his tenth year Baldwin was beaten by policemen in Harlem. The summer when he was fourteen produced "a prolonged religious crisis" in him.[6] Baldwin sought refuge in a church to which one of his young friends had taken him. The woman minister of that church, Bishop Rosa Artemis (Mother) Horn, asked Baldwin on his first trip there, "Whose little boy are you?" Baldwin recalls that the question made him feel so welcome, so wanted, that his heart immediately replied, "Why, yours." In order to escape the ravages of the street, he thus turned to the religious "gimmick" as opposed to the criminal or sexual one. He recognized that

> every Negro boy – in my situation during those years, at least – who reaches this point realizes, at once, profoundly, because he wants to live, that he stands in great peril and must find, with speed, a "thing," a gimmick, to lift him out, to start him on his way. *And it does not matter what the gimmick is.* It was this last realization that terrified me and – since it revealed that the door opened on so many dangers – helped to hurl me into the church.[7]

His transformation/conversion is mirrored in the experience of the young John Grimes in *Go Tell It on the Mountain.* Baldwin recalls:

> [W]hen this woman had finished preaching, everything came roaring, screaming, crying out, and I fell to the ground before the altar. It was the strangest sensation I have ever had in my life – up to that time, or since. I had not known that it was going to happen, or that it could happen. One moment I was on my feet, singing and clapping and, at the same time, working out in my head the plot of a play I was working

on then; the next moment, with no transition, no sensation of falling, I was on my back, with the lights beating down into my face and all the vertical saints above me. I did not know what I was doing down so low, or how I had got there. And the anguish that filled me cannot be described. It moved in me like one of those floods that devastate counties, tearing everything down, tearing children from their parents and lovers from each other, and making everything an unrecognizable waste. All I really remember is the pain, the unspeakable pain; it was as though I were yelling up to Heaven and Heaven would not hear me. And if Heaven would not hear me, if love could not descend from heaven – to wash me, to make me clean – then utter disaster was my portion.[8]

Baldwin joined Mother Horn's church and became an ardent follower, so much so that his brother David was somewhat perturbed by the transformation in Jimmy. The older brother was no fun anymore; he did not want to go to movies or engage in any of the other activities common to young boys. The church may have gained a devotee, but David was being denied an engaged, interesting brother.

Baldwin remained in Mother Horn's church until he was seventeen. He served as a "Young Minister"; his youth made him "a much bigger drawing card" than his father, and he "pushed this advantage ruthlessly." At the same time, he "relished the attention and the relative immunity from punishment" that his "new status" gave him.[9] The competition between Baldwin and his father is echoed in *Go Tell It on the Mountain,* when young John Grimes tries to gain an advantage over his father Gabriel by joining the church. Although the novel does not portray John in a minister's role, that is clearly the status into which the saints are hoping he will grow.

Baldwin said he left the church when he realized that all the "sermons" and "tears" and "repentance" and "rejoicing" had "changed nothing." He also became disillusioned with the "gimmick," with the "illusion" and how it was effected. After all those years of avoiding the theater, he asserted, he had actually been in one the whole time. This idea of the black church as theater or performance, especially the more charismatic churches such as the Pentecostal one to which Baldwin belonged, engaged

Baldwin's creative imagination, not only in *Go Tell It on the Mountain,* but in *The Amen Corner* (1968) as well. Hellfire and damnation, or the fear of hell instead of the promise of heaven, was the underlying premise for the church in which Baldwin's religious ideas were shaped. People were to live righteously, literally by biblical injunction, or suffer the disastrous consequences of not having done so. Baldwin finally escaped the physical structure of the church, but the imaginative and spiritual impact remained with him throughout his writing career. More immediately, these shaping forces informed *Go Tell It on the Mountain.* Baldwin originally entitled the novel *Crying Holy,* then *In My Father's House;* he alternated the titles off and on through 1951.

Baldwin began serious work on his first novelistic venture after he moved to Greenwich Village permanently in 1943 (he had lived there intermittently before). He worked as a waiter at the Calypso, a small restaurant on MacDougal Street owned by Connie Williams.[10] With encouragement from Williams and others, Baldwin waited tables during the day and wrote at night.

A happy meeting with Richard Wright enabled Baldwin to make progress on *In My Father's House.* A young woman who heard Baldwin read a few pages of the novel in the Village introduced him to Wright. When Baldwin visited Wright in Brooklyn in 1945, Wright asked to see what Baldwin had accomplished thus far on the novel. An excited Baldwin forwarded sixty pages to Wright, who read it within days and decided to help the aspiring young writer. Wright contacted Edward Aswell and recommended Baldwin for a Eugene F. Saxon Foundation Fellowship. That Wright was willing to enlist the aid of his own editor in securing a fellowship for Baldwin reveals the extent of the promise he saw in Baldwin's work; it also portended the bitter disappointment Wright would feel later when he thought Baldwin had betrayed him in his appraisal of *Native Son* (1940).[11] The $500 Saxon Fellowship, awarded in November of 1945, boosted Baldwin's ego and enabled him to meet such literary notables as Frank S. MacGregor, president of Harper's, but it did not bring the result he had expected. When the book was rejected for publication, Baldwin felt keenly that he had not lived up to Wright's expectations.

He put *In My Father's House* in a "duffel bag" and turned to another novelistic project entitled *Ignorant Armies*, based on a 1943 case involving a bisexual man who reportedly brutally killed his wife because of their sexual problems. Baldwin tried to move forward with *Ignorant Armies* just as he was confronting the suicide of his friend Eugene Worth, whom he had met in 1943 and who committed suicide in December of 1946 by jumping off the George Washington Bridge. The death was especially painful for Baldwin because he had been sexually attracted to Worth but had not expressed that desire. Baldwin's personal anguish continued as he lived for a while with the woman he planned to marry. But he broke the engagement and threw the intended wedding ring into the Hudson River near where Worth had jumped. These emotional pressures took their toll and *Ignorant Armies* floundered. (Baldwin later salvaged some of the material for inclusion in *Giovanni's Room* [1956] and *Another Country* [1962].)

Baldwin abandoned the budding novel in part because he felt the need to come to grips with his own sexual identity. His personal dilemma joined hands with his writing and social dilemmas. When he reflected on his inability to establish solidly his own sexual and racial identity, along with other problems – the increasing sexual and societal difficulties of being black in America, encounters with white policemen, prejudice, particularly in New Jersey where he had worked for a while, as well as in the Village – he bought a one-way ticket to Paris with the last of the money he had been awarded earlier in the year by the Rosenwald Foundation. On 11 November 1948, when he was twenty-four, he boarded a plane to Paris.

In Paris without resources, Baldwin worked on *Go Tell It on the Mountain* intermittently over the next four years. He developed pieces from it for publication but could not bring it speedily to conclusion. The story of John and Gabriel Grimes held such a grip on Baldwin's imagination that the novel did not suffice to exorcise it all. At intervals during the ten years of composition,

Baldwin paused to develop segments of the story and parcel them out as separate publications. A story, "The Death of the Prophet," appeared in *Commentary* in 1950; a young male character, Johnnie, tries to come to terms with his father's death. "The Rockpile" first appeared in *Going to Meet the Man* in 1965, but the repeat of characters from *Go Tell It on the Mountain* suggests that the story was written earlier. The story parallels the novel in focusing on Roy's fight and resulting injury. Gabriel and Elizabeth share features from the novel, as does John, but whereas there are two sisters, Ruth and Sarah, in the novel, and Elizabeth is pregnant again, only Delilah appears in "The Rockpile," and there is no mention of a pregnancy, though there is a baby boy named Paul. It is also clear that "The Outing" was drawn from the story Baldwin was developing in *Go Tell It on the Mountain.* "The Outing," lifted from the novel when it was called *Crying Holy,* was published in *New Story* in 1951. The story focuses on a church picnic outing on a boat, to which Gabriel and Elizabeth take Roy and Johnnie, along with a younger sister Lois and an unnamed baby boy. Baldwin hints at the theme of homosexuality in the relationship between Johnnie and David Jackson, but the major focus is on the relationship between Johnnie and Gabriel, whose disapproval of his son is ever apparent. There are nuanced differences between these stories and *Go Tell It on the Mountain,* but the oppressive church and the disapproving father are pervasive.[12]

By 1951, Baldwin had met Lucien Happersberger, who would become a close and intimate friend for the remainder of Baldwin's life. Baldwin left Paris and went to Happersberger's home village in Switzerland, Loèche-les-Bains, to complete the novel during the winter of 1951–52.[13] Now calling his novel *Go Tell It on the Mountain,* Baldwin worked for three months to complete the book, reading sections of the manuscript to Lucien in the evenings when he had finished writing and Lucien had finished painting for the day. On 26 February 1952, Baldwin mailed the manuscript to New York. When Knopf expressed interest in the novel, Baldwin flew to New York, with money borrowed from his friend Marlon Brando, to discuss recommended editorial changes. Leeming points out that William Cole, Knopf's publicity director, was very much in favor of publishing the novel, whereas one of the editors asked if it would not be better "without all the Jesus stuff," a rather telling observation considering the fact that "the Jesus stuff" is the essence of the narrative.

With a $250 advance from Knopf, and the promise of $750 more, Baldwin remained in New York to begin rewriting sections of the book. He completed the revisions and returned the manuscript to Knopf in July of 1952. It was accepted and Baldwin received the additional $750. He returned to Paris on 28 August 1952. The anxious waiting for publication of his first novel ended in February of 1953, when he received an advance copy of *Go Tell It on the Mountain.* The novel appeared in May of 1953, with an enthusiastic comment from the poet Marianne Moore, who applauded the "verisimilitude" Baldwin had achieved in his book.

The Story and Its Reception

To reviewers familiar with Baldwin's family history, the novel may well have read as a rite of exorcism against the tyranny of the father, especially when that familial figure uses the tyranny of the church to bolster his position. The religious playing field with which Baldwin was so familiar is the territory on which young John Grimes works out his difficulties with his father Gabriel in *Go Tell It on the Mountain.* Set in Harlem, the novel pits the intuitive sensibility of the illegitimate John and his mother Elizabeth against the strictures of the straitlaced Gabriel. Considering himself the most righteous of the righteous but unable to realize fully his calling as a minister, Gabriel becomes a kind of "holy handyman," pinch-hitting whenever he is needed. The novel also deals with Gabriel's oldest son by Elizabeth (Roy), Gabriel's sister Florence, his first wife Deborah, and his short-term mistress Esther. Other members of the Grimes family are Sarah and Ruth, John and Roy's younger sisters; Elizabeth is pregnant with a fifth child. The story takes place on the Saturday that John turns fourteen. After a violent confrontation between Roy and Gabriel, during which Elizabeth and Florence try to intervene, the group proceeds to the Temple of the Fire Baptized, where John, with the help of Elisha (a slightly older Sunday School teacher and the church's musician), undergoes an all-night spiritual transformation or conversion. Baldwin surrounds these rather straightforward events with flashbacks of the lives of the "saints" – Gabriel, Florence, Elizabeth. The somberness that pervades the Grimes household and relationships is the somberness of fundamentalist religious people who feel they are not entitled to enjoy this world, but who must live sternly and denyingly in order to achieve the next world. Gabriel makes decisions guaranteed to separate his children from their peers, if not to make them objects of derision. The children learn early that total parental acceptance lies only in following the path he has taken; deviation from it meets with physical punishment when they are younger and dire warnings of heavenly punishment later in life.

In contrast to the situation in Baldwin's family, his counterpart in *Go Tell It on the Mountain*, young John Grimes, is unaware of the fact that he is illegitimate. Without that knowledge, he can only believe that there is something inherent in him, in his personality, that makes his father displeased with him. In making this dramatic choice, Baldwin forces John to search for ways of dealing with his father only in the relational realm instead of within a history that preceded his birth; in order to survive emotionally whole, therefore, John must outsmart his father as best he can. One of the primary conflicts in the novel thus becomes the clash between spirit and intellect, with Gabriel presumably representing the former and John growing into a representation of the latter.

In one incident in the novel, his teacher singles out a very young John for special attention. When the principal visits the classroom and asks whose work is on the blackboard, young John is silent for fear that something is wrong. When the teacher encourages him to speak up and the principal asserts, "You're a very bright boy, John Grimes . . . Keep up the good work,"[14] he glimpses dimly the path by which he might escape his father. Although his father can whip his body and control his actions, things that are visible to him, he cannot control his mind. In that private place of invisible thoughts and the potential for mental escape from physical restraints, John uncovers the key to understanding and working through difficult situations. He initially escapes into the world of ideas – movies and fantasizing – for they are as antithetical to his father's Bible as the world the teachers who approve of him represent.

As the novel develops, perspective of presentation is particularly important. Initially, we see Gabriel from a third person, limited point of view that follows John. Our early view of Gabriel is John's early view, and we are equally critical. We see a hard-working and hard man, humorless, confident that he is taking care of his family and serving God in the manner the Almighty intended. He is intolerant of pleasure and insensitive to loving interactions between parents and children. Sternness pervades his personality as well as the descriptions of him. Not exactly an ogre, but close to it, Gabriel does not evoke pleasant responses from us. Anyone who controls his family so thoroughly, requires acquiescence and obedience so firmly, and seems so intent on living out the role he has designed for himself does not garner very much respect or understanding from readers.

Images that Baldwin uses in the early part of the text reinforce the pervasive darkness of personality and relationships. The Saturday morning cleaning rituals introduce the symbolic dust and grime that have choked off family relationships just as surely as they choke John as he tries to clean:

> The room was narrow and dirty; nothing could alter its dimensions, no labor could make it clean. Dirt was in the walls and the floorboards. . . . Dirt was in every corner, angle, crevice of the monstrous stove, and lived behind it in delirious communion with the corrupted wall. Dirt was in the baseboard that John scrubbed every Saturday. . . . Dirt crawled in the gray mop hung out of the windows to dry. John thought with shame and horror, yet in angry hardness of heart: *He who is filthy, let him be filthy still*. . . . John hated sweeping this carpet, for dust rose, clogging his nose and sticking to his sweaty skin, and he felt that should he sweep it forever, the clouds of dust would not diminish, the rug would not be clean. . . . for each dustpan he so laboriously filled at the doorsill demons added to the rug twenty more; he saw in the expanse behind him the dust that he had raised settling again into the carpet; and he gritted his teeth, already on edge because of the dust that filled

his mouth, and nearly wept to think that so much labor brought so little reward.[15]

These images tie in with the family name, "Grimes," to further reinforce Baldwin's suggestion that something is dreadfully amiss in this family. The idea of Gabriel wallowing in the sins of the world, being locked into the very grime from which he believed himself immune, inserts the first of many ironic contrasts into the text. Traditional connotations of color imagery associated with grime and dirt also evoke blackness, a blackness that Christians usually identify with sin and Satan, thereby capturing two concepts simultaneously. First, Christians generally believe that those who are "born again" have been purified, washed in the blood of the Lamb. Their souls have been made "as white" as snow. To "backslide" from this position, then, is to have one's soul "blackened" by sin. Second, the imagery captures the idea of Satan roasting souls in the fires of hell, with their imagined blackened, sooty, ashy look (though never decomposed bodies). Darkness and grime are generally identified with Satan (in spite of the redness of the fire with which one's soul may burn), and hell is generally conceived of as a dark, preternaturally gloomy place.[16]

Although sin is a dominant theme in the novel, clearly some characters sin more than others, and Baldwin encourages readers to respond to different sins with different degrees of understanding or sympathy. Elizabeth's "sin" of having given birth to John out of wedlock is infinitely less significant than Gabriel's sin of having impregnated and abandoned Esther, who gave birth to Royal, Gabriel's first son. Florence's "sin" of leaving her mother on her deathbed to find a better life in New York is ultimately more forgivable than Gabriel's "sin" of holding John and Elizabeth perennially responsible for what he considers her "fall." We might even argue that, although the white men rape Deborah, Gabriel does an equal amount of – if not more – psychological damage to her, and over a much longer period of time. Believing himself finally free of sin, Gabriel does more damage than any other character in the novel.

Yet, as unlikable as Gabriel may be, perhaps it is only fair to view the circumstances from his perspective as well. Baldwin provides that opportunity in "Gabriel's Prayer," the section of the novel that begins part two, "The Prayers of the Saints." Gabriel was a sinner for so long in his drunkenness and whoring that it is perhaps not unexpected that, once he embraced conversion, he would embrace it in the extreme. He becomes the most righteous of the righteous, the purest of the pure, thereby running the risk of passing judgment on others who do not abide by the same standards by which he measures himself. The *good* thing in this process is that Gabriel does make a change; he finds the strength and the imagination to realize that the self-destructive path he is on is not a viable one, and he takes up another course.

The fervor with which he defends Deborah at the banquet of the twenty-four elders might also be a mark in his favor. He looks very tolerant in a group of fat preachers too satisfied with their own superiority from the masses. Gabriel is still new enough in his faith to challenge their lapses. The warmth with which he initially pursues Deborah might also be another mark in his favor; that is tainted somewhat, however, by his motivation for pursuing her. He sees himself in the role of elevating a fallen woman, which means that he has put pride before love, his self-assigned ability to rescue before any clear-sighted evaluation of the sexual or physical attractiveness of the woman as woman. Deborah becomes a cause, an opportunity to act out a biblical text, instead of a real life human being.

Acting out the biblical text also guides Gabriel in "romancing" Elizabeth. Here is another woman fallen by virtue of sexual violation, so Gabriel plans to lift her. To his credit, he is wonderfully loving of and attentive to both Elizabeth and John in the early stages of the courtship. As Elizabeth recounts, he was the best possible surrogate father she could have imagined for John. Unhesitant in playing the role of uplifter, Gabriel changes only when he senses in Elizabeth that she is perhaps not so appreciative of the "rescue" as he had anticipated. As John grows up, Gabriel directs a portion of that dissatisfaction with Elizabeth onto John, partly because he recognizes that this illegitimate heir is better able to live up to his expectations of a royal son than either the dead Royal or the living Roy. This rankles his pride, that oversized, self-imposed directive that guides his life.

Still, to his credit, Gabriel does provide a home for Elizabeth, and as he proceeds to expand his family, he is a good provider in the sense that he pays the bills and puts food on the table. If this were the only measure by which human relationships were to be judged, or by which men are judged to be good, then Gabriel would pass with flying colors. Unfortunately, such a superficial veneer leaves too much of the intricacy of human life uncovered, and in those areas Gabriel falls short. Nonetheless, readers can still identify with the desire of a man to follow directives in which he believes and to have a son to follow in his footsteps. Those desires are just as American as they are religious, for pulling oneself up "by the bootstraps" and acquiring a comfortable house in the suburbs, with a proper nuclear family in it, has been an essential part of the American Dream for decades.

For all this understanding, however, more sympathy usually accrues to the women and John than to Gabriel. His inability to offer emotional sustenance and nurturing places him into a category of acceptance secondary to John and Elizabeth, both of whose artistic and intellectual senses opt for life instead of living death. Through Richard, John's biological father, Elizabeth had been exposed to the world of books and museums. Her final, most poignant memory of Richard is of him reading a book. Florence, for all her shortcomings as a daughter, is nonetheless altruistic toward Elizabeth and the illegitimate John and tries over the years – often unsuccessfully – to protect them from Gabriel's wrath. Florence's desire to live out a romantic dream by going to New York is an understandable one, and readers do not generally see her bowing before the altar at the tarry service as the deserved punishment of being "brought low" into which Gabriel casts it. Deborah and Esther, both of whom have been used by Gabriel, earn sympathetic responses from readers, one for the long-suffering she endures over a long barren life and the other for the intense suffering that brings her short life to a painful end.

John acquired his artistic and intellectual senses from Elizabeth and from his dead father Richard. John has learned that his intellect can capture the attention of the school principal and he explores the libraries throughout Harlem. He is akin to the young Baldwin, who, the author recounts in many places, grew up holding a book in one hand and the newest Baldwin baby in the other. The life of the mind can help him transcend his father calling him "ugly" and saying that he has "the face of Satan," and to cope with his general hostility toward him. John's story of growing up, of learning to deal with his father's tyranny, therefore, is one that endeared many readers to *Go Tell It on the Mountain*.

Numerous reviewers around the country gave their attention to the novel when it initially appeared; they responded in outlets ranging geographically from New York to the *Chicago Sunday Tribune* and the *San Francisco Chronicle*, and philosophically from the *Christian Science Monitor* to the *New Yorker* and *Catholic World*. Most reviewers responded warmly to the story of the Grimes family and John's quest for a spiritual as well as a secular father. They recognized, first and foremost, the linguistic quality and evocative power of Baldwin's writing. J. Saunders Redding, a seasoned writer and critic, wrote in the *New York Herald-Tribune Book Review*: "Baldwin's style is lucid and free-running but involved. It is a style that shows the man to be keenly sensitive to words."[17] The reviewer for *The Nation* called the novel "mature" and "skillful," agreeing with the evaluation of "skillful" that John Henry Raleigh offered in the *New Republic*. Raleigh also praised Baldwin "for a style rich in metaphor and in a sad eloquence." Implicit in most reviews, but explicit in the one in *Time*, was an appreciation of the church basis for Baldwin's impressive style; *Time*'s reviewer observed that Baldwin "sometimes writes with the powerful rocking rhythms of a storefront-church meeting."

Raleigh also joined other reviewers in commenting on the effective use of flashbacks ("skilful time-shift") in the novel. Harvey Curtis Webster observed in *Saturday Review*: "Mr. Baldwin's first novel is written as skilfully as many a man's fifth essay in fiction. His handling of flashbacks so that they show the past without interrupting the drama of the present is masterful." African-American scholar Richard K. Barksdale, writing in *Phylon*, joined Webster and Raleigh in appreciation of Baldwin's "superbly articulated flashbacks." Barksdale's general conclusion was that Baldwin had "written a very fine first novel."

Several reviewers, among them Redding and the reviewer for *Saturday Review*, recognized the influence on Baldwin of Dostoevsky, Faulkner, and other writers. Ralph Ellison, perhaps because of the publication of *Invisible Man* just the year before *Go Tell It on the Mountain*, appears as the consistent point of departure for evaluating Baldwin's achievement. The *New Yorker* reviewer, one of the few voices of objection to anything in Baldwin's novel, used Ellison as the standard against which he found Baldwin lacking. The reviewer judged Baldwin's "perfections" to be "wooden" and "without vitality," compared to Ellison's work, in spite of the novel's realism. He seemed to locate his criticism in the fact that *Go Tell It on the Mountain*, unlike *Invisible Man* and Dostoevsky's *The Brothers Karamazov*, is "humorless." "Mr. Baldwin's God-intoxicated lecher, with his roving eye and his inflamed conscience, which always arrives on the scene too late, carries farce with him wherever he goes, and if one treats him with Kafkaesque solemnity, the life goes out of him and the spiritual tragedy of his congregation loses a dimension." This voice of dissent almost sounds whiny in the context of all the wonderful praise heaped on Baldwin's first novelistic effort; but even this reviewer recognized the "quite exceptional promise" that Baldwin showed in the novel. The only other negative reaction came from Langston Hughes, by this time a well-known writer in his own right. Although Hughes sent a supportive comment when Knopf requested it for the novel, in a letter to Arna Bontemps he voiced his personal doubts about Baldwin's achievement. Hughes criticized *Go Tell It on the Mountain* for not having been written by Zora Neale Hurston, who could have used "her feeling for the folk idiom" to make it "a *quite* wonderful book." Instead, he observed, Baldwin "overwrites and overpoeticizes in images way over the heads of the folks supposedly thinking them." His final conclusion was that *Go Tell It on the Mountain* was "a low-down story in a velvet bag – and a Knopf binding."[18]

Baldwin wrote of the novel that his intention was to focus on people who happened to be Negroes, not exclusively on Negroes.

He asserted that the novel "is a fairly deliberate attempt to break out of what I always think of as the 'cage' of Negro writing. I wanted my people to be people first, Negroes almost incidentally."[19] Reviewers such as Redding accepted that evaluation but others – those writing for *The Commonweal, Time,* and the *New Republic* – clearly did not consider Baldwin the best authority on his accomplishment in the novel as it related to the issue of "Negroes" versus "people." Redding observed of John Grimes that "the fact of his being a Negro has little significance other than as description. John could have been any susceptible fifteen-year-old, illegitimate boy, hated by his stepfather, estranged by younger children from his mother, and forced to live within himself." By contrast, T. E. Cassidy in *The Commonweal* maintained that Baldwin had "not really accomplished" his objective of minimizing race, "because there is always the absolute feeling of injustice toward a people, not just as people, but as a race of people. The disasters that occur are those that occur only, or largely, because these are Negro people." The reviewer for *Time* rejected Baldwin's claim out of hand: "People they certainly are, but so movingly and intensely Negro that any reader listening to them with the compassion Baldwin evokes will overlook his cliché."

The theme of suffering in the novel drew commentary from reviewers almost as consistently as Gabriel's destructive character. The consequences of sin and of racial oppression were the twin prongs causing that suffering. John's plight within this larger context earned John the support of almost all reviewers. Baldwin succeeded in drawing effectively the dilemma of an intelligent young man, on the verge of sexual and spiritual awakening, who cannot trust the person who should be his guide through both these processes.

The Thematic Tradition

In its treatment of the influence of black fundamentalist religious traditions on African-American literature, *Go Tell It on the Mountain* shares kinship with literary works that preceded it and anticipates others that follow it. As Richard K. Barksdale and Keneth

Kinnamon point out in *Black Writers of America,* their comprehensive anthology of African-American literature, the appeal of Christianity was one of the primary preoccupations of black American writers for the first century and a half of composition.[20] The camp meeting phenomenon from the 1740s onward found as many African-Americans attracted to Protestant Western religious traditions as Euro-Americans. Phillis Wheatley thanked the fates that had delivered her in the 1760s from a heathen Africa to a Christian – even though slaveholding – America.[21] Frederick Douglass recognized the appeal of Christianity in his 1845 narrative, even as he proclaimed that the worst fate for an enslaved person was to have a so-called Christian master.[22]

From the time of their introduction to Christianity, African-Americans tended toward the more expressionistic sects, particularly Methodist and Baptist, and these denominations grew rapidly after the Civil War. The concept of God as an anthropomorphic being who listened and responded to His children led black people to take their burdens to the Lord, to express their feelings openly and honestly, and to shout out their happiness in the Lord in reaction to their frustrations in the world. The spirituals as they developed proclaimed that God would hear prayer, that He would not leave motherless children alone, that supplicants could cry out before His altar and He would listen sympathetically and responsively to them. "Nobody knows de trouble I've seen," one such spiritual declared, with the underlying implication that no one in *this* world knows, but certainly God does. "Soon-a will be done with de troubles of the world," another declared, in the hope of going "home to live with God." Still other lines and titles reflected the sense of world-weary travelers who, like John Grimes and his family, could only ease their burdens by bowing down before the throne of God and waiting for deliverance: "There is not a friend like the lowly Jesus. . . . No, not one; no, not one," "Swing low, sweet chariot, coming for to carry me home," "Jesus will fix it."

Fundamentalist African-American churches became sites for exorcising the troubles of the world, and the folk religion became one in which an ever-present God could punish as well as offer mercy. James Weldon Johnson captures the two-pronged tradition vividly in *God's Trombones: Seven Negro Sermons in Verse.*[23] On the one hand, God is the loving, nurturing, mother image as presented in "Go Down, Death: A Funeral Sermon," when He sends Death on a pale horse to bring Sister Caroline "home" to Him. She has borne the heat and the burden of the day, so this personalized delivery to Jesus is her just reward: He wipes away her tears and rocks her in His arms. On the other hand, a misstep from the straight and narrow path can lead to God's unrelenting wrath, as in "The Judgment Day": "Too late, sinner! Too late!/ Good-bye, sinner! Good-bye!/ In hell, sinner! In hell!/ Beyond the reach of the love of God." It is assuredly the fear of hell with which John Grimes awakens on the morning of his fourteenth birthday, and it is equally the fear of death and hell that brings Florence to her knees when she is resistant to bowing. Elizabeth and Gabriel, in varying degrees, are similarly trying to escape the punishment they have been taught is inevitable for the sins they have committed.

A contemporary of James Weldon Johnson's, Nella Larsen, also showed the power of the fundamentalist religious tradition in African-American communities. In *Quicksand* (1928) her protagonist Helga Crane confronts the possibility of experiencing hellfire and damnation. Helga, a middle-class mulatto woman of the Harlem Renaissance, who has taught in an historically black college, been a traveling companion to a prominent woman lecturer, become intimately involved in the nightlife of Harlem, and traveled to Copenhagen to visit white relatives on her father's side, ends up in almost the same position as Elizabeth Grimes. Rejected by the man she loves, Helga stumbles during a rainstorm into a church not unlike the Temple of the Fire Baptized. As she weeps, the parishioners think she is having a religious experience and encourage her to "Come to Jesus." Her clothing makes them view her as a "scarlet 'oman" and a "pore los' Jezebel."[24] She cries out and is "saved"; escorted home by the Reverend Mr. Pleasant Green, a visiting preacher from Alabama, she seduces him, perhaps in an attempt to reclaim the attractiveness her earlier rejection seemingly denied. Faced with what it means to be a woman who has "sinned," who has sunk low in the estimation of her peers and relatives, Helga embraces the fundamentalist church, marries the reverend, and returns with him to Alabama. This progression not only permanently stifles her imagination, but effectively ends her life (she is pregnant with her fifth child at the end of the novel and some readers interpret the delivery as causing literal death for Helga). Combining features of the scarlet woman (Esther in Baldwin's novel) and the long-suffering wife (Elizabeth), Helga never truly realizes her full potential or achieves a clear sense of self. For Larsen, the fundamentalist black church might have offered much to a certain portion of the African-American population, but it effectively kills women like Helga. For women like Helga and Elizabeth, the church is as much quicksand as the racial and gender restrictions that are placed on them.

For the overwhelming majority of the African-Americans involved in fundamentalist churches, however, the attractions outweighed the disadvantages; the institution was as much a social phenomenon as it was religious. Historically, church services could go on all day on Sunday – from Sunday school in the morning, through the eleven o'clock service and after-church dinner, into the evening service – with time allotted in between for church members to visit among themselves. Foot-washings were special occasions for these extended gatherings.[25] Sister McCandless and Sister Price see the Temple of the Fire Baptized as an occasion for socializing with Elizabeth as well as for singing and praising the Lord. And remember that Baldwin even allowed his saints in various manifestations of the Grimes story to go on outings like picnics. The church was where – under the careful supervision of their elders – young people would meet future husbands and wives. When Elisha and Ella Mae are chastised publicly for " 'walking disorderly,' " John realizes that "if they came together again it would be in wedlock. They would have children and raise them in the church."[26]

The idea that such churches regulated private lives led to such practices as young girls who became pregnant out of wedlock having to go before entire congregations, beg pardon for their sin, and ask formally to be reinstated into the church. If the church is viewed as having ever-present eyes on the lives of its members, how much more strongly must the members believe that God, whose "eye is on the sparrow," is watching and judging them. The moral dilemmas of Baldwin's characters, therefore, are grounded in a long history of social reality and literary tradition. The site on which Baldwin chose to work out the intra-familial problems of the Grimes family was a site that African-American readers would instantly recognize, even if they did not totally identify with it.

Baldwin's companion in the 1950s in showing the impact of fundamentalist religious belief on African-American character was Lorraine Hansberry. In *A Raisin in the Sun* (1959), she depicted Mama Lena Younger, a matriarch in her sixties who has held her family together with prayer and sheer force of will. A representation of what an Elizabeth Grimes might grow into, Mama Lena wants her children to remain safely in the hollow of the hand of the Lord. When her college-aged daughter Beneatha reasserts her desire to be a doctor, Mama Lena agrees that, "God willing," Beneatha will achieve her objective. When Beneatha denies the significance of God and declares, "There simply is no blasted God – there is only man and it is he who makes miracles!," that blasphemy is more than Mama Lena can stand. She powerfully slaps her daughter and insists that she repeat after her: "In my mother's house, there is still God."[27]

I call that scene "Christianity's last stand" in African-American literature. Representations of religious experience by black American writers of the 1970s and 1980s, following the impact of the Black Arts Movement and the tenets of the Black Aesthetic, would be transformed dramatically. This is striking in Ntozake Shange's *For Colored Girls Who Have Considered Suicide When the Rainbow is Enuf,* where the women declare at the end of the play, "i found god in myself/ & i loved her/ i loved her fiercely," and in Toni Morrison's *Beloved* (1987), where formerly enslaved Baby Suggs, a far removed descendant of Gabriel Grimes, takes to her "pulpit" to teach – without a biblical text – that black people should simply learn to love themselves and each other.[28] What would have been blasphemy for Baldwin's characters becomes for his descendants a way of creating space for black women to grow, to know and define themselves, and for black people to expand their perceptions of what it means to exist in a universe that does not have damning them as one of its foremost objectives. In this continuum of literary representation of black religious experience, therefore, *Go Tell It on the Mountain* stands out as a singular moment in literary history as well as in literary achievement.

The Critical Tradition

Go Tell It on the Mountain has remained the primary novel through which readers come to Baldwin's works. Generations of scholars have praised the novel for a variety of reasons. The hard-to-please Robert A. Bone, writing in 1965, cited *Go Tell It on the Mountain* as superior to anything Baldwin had written to that point. Judging it "very good indeed," Bone was lavish in identifying strengths of the novel: "This is Baldwin's earliest world, his bright and morning star, and it glows with metaphorical intensity. Its emotions are his emotions; its language, his native tongue. The result is a prose of unusual power and authority."[29] Throughout its forty-three-year history, the novel has garnered praise for the power of the language that has become Baldwin's signature – its repetitious constructions, its realism, its evocative force, its almost hypnotic effect.

Responsive to the power of Baldwin's narrative of a working class family immersed in fundamentalist religious traditions, many critics have found their thematic points of departure in Baldwin's use of church traditions – the power of the rhetoric as well as the impact of belief or lack of belief on the characters in the text. Two of the earliest and still often-cited such treatments are Shirley S. Allen's "Religious Symbolism and Psychic Reality in Baldwin's *Go Tell It on the Mountain*" and Edward Margolies' "The Negro Church: James Baldwin and the Christian Vision."[30] Critics as wide-ranging in interpretive postures as Stanley Macebuh, Louis H. Pratt, and Michel Fabre have similarly found Baldwin's church-based text inviting to discussion, not only for its intrinsic worth but for what it reveals about Baldwin himself. The general consensus is that Baldwin uses the novel to work out his own uncertainties about the religious tradition in which he grew up.[31] More recently, Trudier Harris has argued that in the novel the church imprisons the black women characters and creates in them a sense of guilt so profound they will never achieve true self-realization and introspection.[32]

As a coming-of-age protagonist, John Grimes has received treatment as a young man estranged from his earthly father as well as from his heavenly Father, and as a young man both attracted to and repelled by the prospect of homosexual desire. Although the latter theme is one that may be implicit in many critical studies of *Go Tell It on the Mountain,* it has been treated rather gingerly, as in John S. Lash's brief study.[33] In more recent years, gay theorists have turned to Baldwin's works to claim him or to complain about his representation of homosexuality; this is especially true in Lee Edelman's exploration of what he perceives as Baldwin's difficulties with his sexual and racial identities.[34]

A couple of book-length studies of Baldwin's works, with appropriate treatments of *Go Tell It on the Mountain,* are in the tradition of formula studies and have been published by the houses that sponsored them.[35] Baldwin's relationship to Norman Mailer inspired one study,[36] but the overall number of thematic or sustained critical studies has perhaps lagged behind the number for American writers with literary corpuses comparable to that of Baldwin. Among the critical studies on Baldwin Horace Porter's *Stealing the Fire: The Art and Protest of James Baldwin* (1989) is noteworthy.[37] Other book-length treatments are compilations of essays, including *James Baldwin: A Collection of Critical Essays* (1974), *James Baldwin: A Critical Evaluation* (1977), and *Critical Essays on James Baldwin* (1988).[38]

Baldwin's death in December of 1987 evoked – as might be expected – much new critical interest. This manifested itself in the production of a documentary film on Baldwin entitled *The Price of the Ticket,* along with a couple of collections of essays (one in honor of Baldwin), and a book of *Conversations With James Baldwin.* In one collection, edited by Quincy Troupe, internationally known writers Wole Soyinka, Toni Morrison, Maya Angelou, William Styron, Chinua Achebe, and a host of others comment on Baldwin's works, their friendships with him, and his place in African-American and American letters.[39] Baldwin's death also hastened completion of his "official" biography. David Leeming, who had worked as Baldwin's secretary for a number of years and was authorized to write the biography, published *James Baldwin: A Biography* in 1994.[40] Full of details of Baldwin's national and international activities and interactions with the famous, the infamous, and the ordinary, Leeming's volume goes considerably further than the formula studies. Other biographies of the writer who took it upon himself to become America's conscience will surely be forthcoming.

In recent years, as more and more African-American women writers have become increasingly popular, and as their subject matter has come to encompass the supernatural and the fantastic, students have had to learn how to re-read novels like Baldwin's *Go Tell It on the Mountain,* with its primary emphasis on character and plights of the soul. The essays in the current volume are designed to assist that process; they bring new insights to a novel that has remained in print consistently and been consistently read since its publication in 1953. Michael F. Lynch picks up where many previous critics began, with an examination of the theology and Christianity that inform *Go Tell It on the Mountain.* Lynch expands these viewpoints by highlighting the dialectical pairs that made Baldwin's first novel much more than a study in secular/sacred opposition. Horace Porter argues that the South serves as the epitome of repressive physical and psychological horror for Baldwin. It not only informs the tension between Gabriel and John, but its negative connotations, which Baldwin derived in part from his knowledge of his father's origins, become a shaping and recurring metaphor in Baldwin's creative imagination. Bryan R. Washington takes to task gay theorists who use Baldwin's novel to work out preconceived expectations for African-American literature and who assert that Baldwin, reluctant to identify himself as a "gay writer," is himself racist and homophobic. Shifting personal identities and the multiple layers of narrative that make all presumed absolute categories unstable are the perspectives from which Vivian M. May examines male and female character in the novel. Finally, Keith Clark articulates a paradigmatic quest for male communitas of which there are glimpses in *Go Tell It on the Mountain,* a quest that falls short of fruition. He discusses Baldwin's desire to achieve communitas with other black male writers and intellectuals, which he apparently realized only briefly during his early days in Paris.

These aspiring and established scholars make it clear that the issues and themes raised in *Go Tell It on the Mountain* will continue to inspire and engage the most sophisticated forms of critical evaluation and interpretation.

NOTES

1 James Baldwin, *Notes of a Native Son* (Boston: Beacon Press, 1955; rpt: Bantam, 1968), p. 77.

2 James Baldwin, *Go Tell It on the Mountain* (New York: Knopf, 1953; rpt: New York: Dell, 1974), p. 36.

3 Baldwin, "Interview with Inmates at Riker's Island Prison in New York," *Essence* (June 1976), p. 55.

4 Baldwin, *Notes of a Native Son,* pp. 72, 73.

5 Baldwin, *Notes of a Native Son,* p. 73.

6 Baldwin, *The Fire Next Time* (New York: Dial, 1963; rpt. Laurel, 1963), p. 27.

7 Baldwin, *The Fire Next Time,* pp. 37–38; emphasis in original.

8 Baldwin, *The Fire Next Time,* pp. 44–45.

9 Baldwin, *The Fire Next Time,* p. 48.

10 David Leeming traces the development of the novel across several of the chapters in *James Baldwin: A Biography* (New York: Knopf, 1994). I am indebted to him for many of the details in the following paragraphs.

11 In two separate essays, Baldwin complains about the protest tradition and Wright's portrayal of Bigger Thomas in *Native Son.* See "Everybody's Protest Novel" and "Many Thousands Gone," both of which were collected in *Notes of a Native Son* (1955).

12 I discuss the connections between "The Rockpile," "The Outing," and *Go Tell It on the Mountain* in *Black Women in the Fiction of James Baldwin* (Knoxville: University of Tennessee Press, 1985), ch. 2.

13 Baldwin discusses his reception in that all-white environment in "Stranger in the Village," originally published in *Harper's* in Octo-

ber, 1953, and reprinted in *Notes of a Native Son* (1955). Forced to come to grips with his blackness in the midst of unintentional racial slurs and curiosity in the Village and stressed by a desperate need to finish the novel, Baldwin found that listening to the music of Bessie Smith reconciled him "to being a Nigger."

14 Baldwin, *Go Tell It on the Mountain,* p. 20.

15 Baldwin, *Go Tell It on the Mountain,* pp. 21, 22, 26–27; emphasis in original.

16 It is ironic that African-Americans, themselves *black,* have adopted so readily the traditional color symbolism assigned to Christian religious belief. This is especially relevant in Gabriel's and John's cases, because their senses of self are so fragile, and since Gabriel so readily associates white people with "evil," not with the purity of religious color imagery that so contradictorily informs his life and identity.

17 Quotations from reviews in this paragraph and throughout the text are taken from the following sources: J. Saunders Redding, "Sensitive Portrait of a Lonely Boy," *New York Herald-Tribune Book Review* (May 17, 1953), p. 5; T. E. Cassidy, "The Long Struggle," *The Commonweal* 58 (May 22, 1953): 186; *The Nation* 176 (June 6, 1953): 488; John Henry Raleigh, "Messages and Sagas," *New Republic* 128 (June 22, 1953): 21; *New Yorker* 29 (June 20, 1953): 93; *Time* 61 (May 18, 1953): 126–127; *Saturday Review* 36 (May 16, 1953): 14; and Richard K. Barksdale, "Temple of the Fire Baptized," *Phylon* 14 (1953): 326–327. Other journals and newspapers that reviewed the novel in 1953 include: *The New York Times* (May 17, 1953), p. 5; *The Christian Science Monitor* (May 28, 1953), p. 11; *The San Francisco Chronicle* (July 5, 1953), p. 18; *Booklist* 49 (March 15, 1953): 229; *Catholic World* 177 (August 1953): 393; *Chicago Sunday Tribune* (July 12, 1953), p. 7; *Kirkus* 21 (April 1, 1953): 331; *Library Journal* 78 (May 15, 1953): 916; *Springfield Republican* (July 19, 1953), p. 7D; *U.S. Quarterly Book Review* 9 (Spring 1953): 297; and *Yale Review* 42 (Summer 1953): 10.

18 Langston Hughes to Arna Bontemps, 18 February 1953, in Charles Nichols, ed., *The Letters of Langston Hughes and Arna Bontemps,* p. 302. As Arnold Rampersad points out in his biography of Langston Hughes, Hughes was not pleased that Knopf had recently essentially dropped him as an author by refusing to publish his selected poems after the poor reception to *Montage of a Dream Deferred.* See *The Life of Langston Hughes Volume II: 1941–1967* (New York: Oxford University Press, 1988), p. 205.

19 James Baldwin; quoted in T. E. Cassidy, "The Long Struggle," *The Commonweal* 58 (May 22, 1953): 186.

20 Richard Barksdale and Keneth Kinnamon, *Black Writers of America: A Comprehensive Anthology* (New York: Macmillan, 1972), p. 2.

21 See "On Being Brought from Africa to America," in *The Poems of Phillis Wheatley,* ed. Julian Mason (Chapel Hill: The University of North Carolina Press, 1989), p. 53.

22 *Narrative of the Life of Frederick Douglass: An American Slave, Written by Himself,* ed. Benjamin Quarles (1845; rpt.: Cambridge: Harvard University Press, 1960).

23 James Weldon Johnson, *God's Trombones: Seven Negro Sermons in Verse* (New York: Viking, 1927).

24 Nella Larsen, *Quicksand* (1928: rpt: New York: Collier, 1971), p. 187.

25 Foot-washings occur specifically in Primitive Baptist churches. In literal imitation of Christ, members kneel before each other and wash each other's feet. Depending on the size of the congregation, this procedure could take some time, and often other churches of the same denomination would be invited to share in such rituals. Usually all-day occasions, these gatherings include on-the-grounds cooking and eating, extensive visiting, and recreational activities as long-lasting as softball games. On these Sundays, all participants in the foot-washings usually wear white. Again, the social significance of such gatherings is as important as the religious significance.

26 Baldwin, *Go Tell It on the Mountain,* p. 17.

27 Lorraine Hansberry, *A Raisin in the Sun* (1959; rpt: New York: Signet, 1966), p. 39.

28 Ntozake Shange, *For Colored Girls Who Have Considered Suicide When the Rainbow is Enuf* (New York: Bantam, 1977), p. 67, and Toni Morrison, *Beloved* (New York: Knopf, 1987).

29 Robert A. Bone, *The Negro Novel in America* (rev. ed., New Haven: Yale University Press, 1965), pp. 218–219.

30 Shirley S. Allen, "Religious Symbolism and Psychic Reality in Baldwin's *Go Tell It on the Mountain,*" *CLA Journal* 19 (1975): 173–199 and Edward Margolies, *Native Sons: A Critical Study of Twentieth-Century Negro American Authors* (New York: Lippincott, 1968), pp. 102–126.

31 Stanley Macebuh, *James Baldwin: A Critical Study* (New York: Third World Press/Joseph Okpaku, 1973); Louis H. Pratt, *James Baldwin* (Boston: Twayne Publishers, 1978); Michel Fabre, "Father and Sons in James Baldwin's *Go Tell It on the Mountain,*" in *James Baldwin: A*

Collection of Critical Essays, ed. Keneth Kinnamon (Englewood Cliffs, NJ: Prentice-Hall, 1974).

32 Trudier Harris, *Black Women in the Fiction of James Baldwin* (1985).

33 John S. Lash, "Baldwin Beside Himself: A Study in Modern Phallicism," *CLA Journal* 7 (December 1964): 132–140.

34 Lee Edelman, "The Part for the (W)hole: Baldwin, Homophobia, and the Fantasmatics of 'Race,' " in *Homographesis: Essays in Gay Literary and Cultural Theory* (New York: Routledge, 1994), pp. 42–75.

35 See Carolyn Wedin Sylvander, *James Baldwin* (New York: Ungar, 1980), and Pratt, *James Baldwin*.

36 W. J. Weatherby, *Squaring Off: Mailer vs. Baldwin* (New York: Mason/Charter, 1977).

37 Horace Porter, *Stealing the Fire: The Art and Protest of James Baldwin* (Middletown, CT: Wesleyan University Press, 1989).

38 Kinnamon, ed., *James Baldwin: A Collection of Critical Essays;* Therman B. O'Daniel, ed., *James Baldwin: A Critical Evaluation* (Washington, D.C.: Howard University Press, 1977, 1981); Fred L. Standley and Nancy V. Burt, eds., *Critical Essays on James Baldwin* (Boston: G. K. Hall, 1988). Seasoned Baldwin scholar Fred L. Standley, along with Nancy V. Standley, also completed *James Baldwin: A Reference Guide* (Boston: G. K. Hall, 1980).

39 Quincy Troupe, ed., *James Baldwin: The Legacy* (New York: Simon & Schuster, 1989); Jules Chametzsky, ed., *Black Writers Redefine the Struggle: A Tribute to James Baldwin* (Amherst: The University of Massachusetts Press, 1989); Fred L. Standley and Louis H. Pratt, eds., *Conversations With James Baldwin* (Oxford: University Press of Mississippi, 1989).

40 Earlier, Fern Marja Eckman had interviewed Baldwin extensively in preparation for *The Furious Passage of James Baldwin* (New York: M. Evans and Co., 1966). Her work is particularly good in tying the details of Baldwin's life to *Go Tell It on the Mountain*.

2

A Glimpse of the Hidden God: Dialectical Vision in Baldwin's *Go Tell It on the Mountain*

MICHAEL F. LYNCH

Just above my head
I hear music in the air
And I really do believe
There's a God somewhere.
(gospel song)

The whole question . . . of religion has always really obsessed me.
A Rap on Race 83

I

JAMES Baldwin is most commonly viewed in both the popular mind and the scholarly community as the eloquent voice of black rage of the 1960s and the prophet of black exasperation with the failures of the civil rights movement as expressed in the rebellions in the cities. The virtual association of Baldwin with black militancy and, at its extreme, the spirit of black vengeance of the late 60s is highly ironic, however, when one considers Baldwin's insistence that hatred of any kind amounts to self-destruction and that the individual bears responsibility to himself or herself for attaining self-knowledge and to others for offering reconciliation and love. Given his considerable, understandable anger, his explicit role as witness for African-Americans, and his exaggerated image as the enraged prophet of retribution, Baldwin would seem perhaps the least likely writer to assert the redemptive power of suffering, partly because such an association would contribute to the misperception that he was retro-

Research for this essay was assisted by a summer fellowship from the Virginia Foundation for the Humanities and by a research activity appointment from Kent State University.

grade and reactionary. Yet he expands that theme implicitly through the early novels, plays, and essays, and through his middle and later work he continues to explore it despite considerable risk and damage to his reputation. In the late 60s and early 70s, when radical rhetoric and action among young black leaders supplanted the less confrontational, less inflammatory approach of Martin Luther King, Jr. and his successors, Baldwin was in fact reviled for his emphasis on individuality and personality instead of radical ideology, and for his failure to endorse violence as a primary tool in the revolutionary movement.

Ironically, at the same time Baldwin was being scorned by the new black leaders for his insufficiently radical agenda, he was also being indicted by the critical establishment for an apparent endorsement of violence, an alleged obsession with pointless rage, a despairing and even hateful vision, and a rapid, precipitous decline in both content and craft. Baldwin was especially vulnerable to attacks from such polarized positions because he did not accept the apparent contradiction of such dualities and actually strove to reconcile them. The standard critical charge against his later work, motivated it seems in part by both conservative distaste for his "message" and liberal vexation with his intensified critique of liberal "solutions," is that after the mid-60s his writing loses its irony, complexity, and artistic command of language and declines rapidly from rich, eloquent ambiguity to relatively sterile, polemical diatribe. Although there are some artistic problems with his later writing, this charge proceeds from a polarizing viewpoint which fails to apprehend Baldwin's increasingly subtle fusion of a political perspective with a personalist one.

The most pervasive problem with Baldwin criticism is this projection of a dichotomized schema onto an artist whose method is fundamentally dialectical. Whereas the former approach finds opposing ideas mutually exclusive, an either-or, the latter recognizes that beneath the apparent contradiction lies a dynamic inner tension and interconnection, striving to reconcile the conflict by exploring the truth of both positions. Much of the response to Baldwin's work privileges the artificial separation and contraposition of what are actually interdependent, mutually reinforcing realities, creating an oversimplified, confining understanding of a writer who celebrates contradictions wedded and made intelligible through paradox.[1] Dialectical thinking such as Baldwin's tends to yield irony, restraint, open-mindedness, and a reluctance to judge others – all qualities for which he was generally praised until the early or mid-60s. The inaccurate charge that he polemicizes his writing from that point on is rooted in critics' positing the individual and/or spiritual over against the political, an opposition Baldwin attempts to reconcile. In my view, his later work achieves more complexity than the prevailing assessment contends because he does not become a polemicist and because as a dialectical thinker he continues to respect and maintain the necessary vital tension between spiritual vision and political reality. There are three key dialectical pairs in Baldwin's work, which are often misrepresented as dualistic oppositions instead of interdependent terms: first, his revolt against Christianity based on his internalization of Christian precepts, together with his individual quest for faith and God; second, his agitation for social justice and political freedom, together with his insistence on a person's responsibility for his or her own individual, spiritual freedom; and third, his identity as an American, together with his sense of racial identity as a black person. This article will discuss briefly the first of these dialectical pairs and then consider *Go Tell It on the Mountain* as it reflects Baldwin's complex relationship with Christianity and faith.

A corollary of the overemphasis placed on Baldwin's political intent has been the neglect of the other term of his dialectic, his personalist or spiritual perspective, which also figures as a dominant and consistent concern in his work. In *A Rap on Race* Baldwin, in a rare moment of explicit candor about his lifelong absorption with matters spiritual, tells Margaret Mead that "The whole question . . . of religion has always really obsessed me" (*A Rap on Race*, hereafter RR: 83). Baldwin's fundamentally Christian but individualized, occasionally unorthodox theology permeates his work, including the much maligned later fiction and essays, in which he is supposed to betray the ideal of love for virtually nihilistic hatred and self-pity. Yet the overwhelming critical tendency to attempt to dichotomize Baldwin's thought, combined with the privileging of social and political analysis over that of craft and art, so common in the treatment of works by black writers, has prevented substantial analysis of a major aspect of his thought and art.[2] It also seems that the increasing stridency of his critique of Christendom, including both the white and the black churches, has discouraged close examination of his implicit religious faith. In spite of the profusion of biblical allusions and Christian symbols and themes throughout Baldwin's writing, the scholarship, aside from brief mention of the residual Christian content of his imagery, his preacherly rhythms, and his role as an Old Testament prophet, has offered no sustained treatment of his religious thought or theology. It seems to be generally assumed either that Baldwin has no theology or that it does not matter because he left the church. He is generally regarded as an apostate who uses religious images, with the rhythms and rhetoric he learned as a teen preacher, simply because he cannot help himself. Contrary to the prevailing critical view, however, Baldwin's investment in Christian ideals and themes did not end when he abandoned his role as preacher in a Harlem fundamentalist church at age seventeen. Although Baldwin bitterly attacks Christianity over the course of his career for what he sees as its condoning of racism and injustice toward blacks, he developed a theology based on Christian ideals and on his individual quest for a loving God.

Baldwin grew up in the black fundamentalist church, where his father served as an assistant minister and James gained a profound sense of his own power and potential in serving as a successful preacher from the ages of fourteen to seventeen. *The Fire Next Time* contains an account of the factors that drew the adolescent into the church and the pulpit, including his fear of not surviving his Harlem environment, his sense of personal depravity, and his desperate need for "a gimmick" (*The Fire Next Time,* hereafter FNT: 38) and a source of leverage against his harsh father. Baldwin explains that "all the fears with which I had grown up, and which were now a part of me and controlled my vision of the world, rose up like a wall between the world and me, and drove me into the church" (FNT 41). In addition to the predominantly secular motives and the cynical behavior he observes, especially among the clergy, Baldwin locates the major source of his disillusionment in the church's failure to apply the Christian principle of universal love:

> There was no love in the church. It was a mask for hatred and self-hatred and despair. . . . When we were told to love everybody, I had thought that that meant *everybody*. But no. It applied only to those who believed as we did, and it did not apply to white people at all. (FNT 53–54)

He tells how his father slapped him when he brought home a Jewish friend who was not "saved" and who therefore would burn for eternity. The young minister's response to his father, "He's a better Christian than you are" (FNT 51), epitomizes his rejection of the church on Christian grounds and foreshadows his lifelong search for an ideal of love outside the church. In *Go Tell It on the Mountain* Baldwin indicts the black fundamentalist church for its image of a vengeful, unforgiving God and for the consequent deforming effects on its members, whose entrapment in guilt and fear prevents them from loving themselves or others. Baldwin objects especially to the awful sense of doom and the inevitability of punishment and perdition infused into the faithful. *The Amen Corner,* written shortly after *Go Tell It on the Mountain,* intensifies the attack on the church, following John Grimes's ambiguous conversion with David Alexander's explicit loss of faith which constitutes his coming of age. Margaret, David's mother, has achieved a successful ministry based on self-glorification and abuse of power, but accomplished at the cost of abandoning her husband and neglecting the needs of her son. Underlying much of the divisiveness and pain caused by her ministry is the false dichotomy of the sacred versus the secular and her belief that God punishes people for being too happy. Margaret's eventual conversion from self-righteous power and religiosity to compassion and love of family anticipates the secular religion of love and community which Baldwin evokes in his last two novels.

Whatever his feelings about the Christian church and religion, Baldwin clearly must be considered a theological writer, one who continually wrestles with the identity and meaning of God and whose debt to Christian precepts informs his own evolving vision. His early rescue from the streets by the church, along with his youthful immersion in biblical wisdom and symbology, seems to have instilled in him an unalterable sense of the predominance of spiritual realities and a preoccupying concern with the religious, moral, and psychological aspects of salvation. One might say that Baldwin's work evinces a writer "afflicted" with belief in God as an unshakable burden, an impression suggested by his many characters driven by questions about God's identity as much as their own and haunted by the conflict between their rebellion against and their great need of Him. In addition to a few unusually open comments in interviews regarding his image of God, in places Baldwin admits his assimilation of Christian ideals and even accepts the designation of Christian. In *A Rap on Race,* Mead corners an evasive Baldwin, who reluctantly acknowledges that he derives his concept of morality from Christianity. Citing his mother as "the first Christian I knew," he adds, "Somehow she really made us believe it was more important for us to love each other and love other people than anything else" (RR 85). He notes that many Christians are offended by Christ's being "a very disreputable person" (RR 85), and he identifies Christ's example as the essence of morality: "In my case, in order to become a moral human being, whatever that may be, I have to hang out with publicans and sinners, whores and junkies, and stay out of the temple" (RR 86). When Mead points out that she is not trying to call Baldwin a Christian, he actually allows the identification, saying, "I'll accept the term" (RR 86).

Baldwin spent nearly a decade writing and revising his first novel, *Go Tell It on the Mountain,* and his investment of time and craft has been vindicated over the years with high critical praise. Although scholars tend to agree on the novel as his paramount achievement in fiction and one of his greatest works, most frequently also citing *Notes of a Native Son* and *The Fire Next Time,* they are sharply divided on its treatment of and attitude toward Christian belief. As mentioned above, many critics ignore, minimize, or deny Baldwin's spirituality. But among the few who address the issue in *Go Tell It on the Mountain,* most find the novel an absolute denial of the possibility of belief. For Michel Fabre, the salvation of John Grimes "remains problematical," limited to "a spark without a future. . . . True knowledge is absent, rebirth impossible" (Fabre 133). Fabre dichotomizes and distorts the idea of religion as "either (and this seems to me to be the case) a 'gimmick' which does not provide spiritual salvation" or a mythical panacea whose "efficacious grace redeems everyone" (Fabre 133). Nagueyalti Warren concludes just as emphatically that a religious reading of the novel is a misinterpretation because "one thing is clear; . . . John is not a believer" (Warren 26) and his "faith is lost" (Warren 19). Stanley Macebuh's study, the only book offering some sustained analysis of Baldwin's theology, somehow ignores the central issue of his handling of John's experience on the threshing floor, missing the point with peripheral discussion of John's "discovery of a new, more congenial religion . . . of love" (Macebuh 67). Some critics attempt to read into *Go Tell It on the Mountain* the distorted interpretation of Baldwin's later career which reduces him to a protesting polemicist. Nathan Scott, for example, unable to label the novel as one of outright protest, still claims that it can "be seen in retrospect as marking the path he was increasingly to follow in the years to come" as Baldwin's "own chosen role became more and more to be that of racial ideologue" (Scott 161, 162). Not surprisingly, Scott finds only "the memory of Christianity" (Scott 163) in this novel, where "one could hardly argue that . . . the stuff of experience is being conceived of Christianly" (Scott 162). The nadir of this sort of approach is attained in the argument of Fred Standley, where the novel is not even about religion but is merely "a sociopolitical novel that subtly but savagely indicts a white controlled society'' (Standley, *Critical Essays,* 191).

Only a few scholars identify the affirmative treatment of Christian belief in the novel. Although Donald Gibson's article offers little specific analysis of the novel, he argues for its "ultimate . . . theological meaning" based on the lack of irony or ambiguity in John's epiphany, concluding "that John's experience is truly a Christian one, that the novel is a Christian novel and that it points to what the author conceives to be a sphere beyond the experiential" (Gibson 6). Sondra O'Neale, in the context of her discussion of Baldwin's Christianity and his search for God, notes briefly that *Go Tell It on the Mountain* is a "quasi-religious novel" (O'Neale 132) that illustrates not only "the unremitting oppression" Baldwin received from the world but also "the experiential anointing and ethereal vision" (O'Neale 127) granted to him on the floor of a Harlem church. Shirley Allen's two articles present the only detailed analysis of the novel's "serious attitude toward religious faith" as seen in "the passionate seriousness of John's religious experience" (Allen, "Ironic Voice" 36, 37). Claiming that "those who find the ending of the novel ambiguous fail to catch the echo in Elisha's words of Isaiah's promise, 'They shall run and not be weary,' " she demonstrates that the novel's multiple biblical allusions convey John's "conversion – his understanding and acceptance of the central Christian belief" (Allen, "Symbolism" 169, 175).

Even considering the general disinclination to explore Baldwin's theological preoccupations, it is remarkable how little attention his most accomplished novel has generated in this regard. Of all Baldwin's works, his affirmation of subjective Christian faith and his emotional involvement with the mystery of God are most evident and most intense here. The dialectic of social critique and spiritual vision which informs his other works also permeates and has its roots in *Go Tell It on the Mountain,* and it creates the dynamic tension which accounts for much of the novel's power. O'Neale describes the tension of Baldwin's dialectical position generally as well as his unique, pivotal role in the history of the relationship of African-American writers with Christianity:

> Baldwin should be seen as the last black American writer to exploit as a major theme the black man's relationship with Christianity. Conversely, he may be considered the first black American writer to distance himself from the lone enduring black institution, the black church, not by its notable absence (as with Wright, Ellison, and other blacks writing in the first half of this century) . . . but by his overtly persistent portrayal of its lack of authentic Christian commitment. . . . Baldwin opened the floodgates for contemporary anti-Christian, nonbiblically based black American literature. (O'Neale 140)

With *Go Tell It on the Mountain* Baldwin criticizes the black church and Christianity by illustrating the tragedy of a perverted theology in most of the characters' lives and its construction of a false God. Yet he also asserts a "radical" – in the sense of fundamental or traditional – Christian theology that includes salvation through universal love and forgiveness, the necessity for spiritual death and resurrection, and the hiddenness and risk of authentic faith. John's rebellion against his church's hopeless theology bears fruit in his brief but ecstatic vision of the real God of love.

II

In *Go Tell It on the Mountain* Baldwin censures not Christian theology per se but its misapplication among many of the professed in Christendom. Nor does he target the white church specifically, as he does with considerable stridency in many later works, but the black fundamentalist church, the site of his initiation and early service in the faith. Although the novel includes some sociopolitical elements relative to racial conflict, its treatment of Christianity transcends that issue. Observing the audacity of Baldwin's commentary on the church, which seems to have obscured for many readers the other term of his dialectic, O'Neale notes that "no black American writer before Baldwin had quite the literary nerve (i.e., to risk separating himself from the mainstream of Christian black America) or the agnostic impertinence . . . to question openly the justice, judgment, and sincerity of God" (O'Neale 131). Whereas Richard Wright dismisses all Christian faith as a delusion and an escape from freedom and responsibility, Baldwin's critique is more complex and more powerful because it issues from an agonized belief. Just as Baldwin opposes the aesthetics of literary naturalism as epitomized in Wright's *Native Son,* he challenges the Calvinistic God who created a world sunk in depravity only to delight in the inevitability of its doom. Baldwin portrays his personal "theological terror" (Macebuh 39) with various characters' certainty of falling and horror of damnation. The root of most of the unhappiness and unloving behavior of the characters is their church's image of the Old Testament God consumed with threatening and condemning his creatures. Their consequent religious neurosis becomes evident in their dominant emotions of fear, guilt, and anger, their failure to forgive others or themselves, and their inability to live with any sense of freedom. Mirroring the behavior of their God, they are filled with the desire for vengeance, which they express repeatedly through uttering curses and praying for their enemies' destruction. The predominance of such unhealthy and unholy inclinations tends to produce peak religious experiences or conversions that are essentially extorted, heavily tainted by elements of coercion and/or insincerity, as illustrated by Florence, Gabriel, Elizabeth, and to some extent, even John.

Within the church which formed Baldwin's religious sensibility, therefore, temporal happiness and spiritual redemption are seemingly impossible attainments – largely because, he suggests, they are seen as antithetical terms of a dichotomy. Most of the characters in the novel illustrate the damage caused by the joyless, unnecessary, and unnatural opposition of the secular and the sacred. The pathology of this brand of theology generates self-hatred and rebellion against such a severe God. Baldwin's interest in the theology of revolt can be traced in part to the influence of Wright and Dostoevsky, who examine its dialectical potential for nihilistic self-destruction and healing knowledge of God.[3] The rebellions of Florence and Gabriel, characterized by selfishness and lack of love, end in self-pity and despair. On the other hand, the rebellions of Elizabeth and John, based on their efforts to deny and bridge the secular-sacred dichotomy, are guided by open-hearted questing for the benevolent Father, so that their risking annihilation for this knowledge lends their ventures an heroic aspect. Baldwin also considers those like John's father Richard, Elizabeth's father, and Esther (and to some extent also Royal and Roy), who refuse or break all ties to theology and church yet whose salutary secularity brings them closer to the spirit of God than is possible through such repressive denial.

Although Florence has chosen for most of her life to reject the church's control, she has been influenced by her mother's strict religious nature, experiencing repressed guilt over leaving her, hatred of her brother and all men, and fear for her soul as she nears death (Harris 34). Like John, she has avoided direct confrontation with God, yet she now prostrates herself before him and humbles herself in her brother's reproving sight, out of terror that God is evidently taking her life as revenge for her rebellion. In her weakness she returns to "her mother's starting place, the altar of the Lord" (66), but in her heart, pride as well as "hatred and bitterness weighed like granite" (66). Florence has never forgiven her mother or Gabriel for his appropriation of her birthright, the loss of which was compounded with her mother's curse as Florence abandoned her many years ago. Gabriel has exploited his mother's cherished theological theme of God's unfailing promises for his own self-glorification, but Florence has renounced it throughout her life, bitterly demanding everything but never hoping for much of anything. She faces the altar, angry at the image of God she has refused to serve, "divided between a terrible longing to surrender and a desire to call God into account" (90). Her gesture of defiance and rage against him, as she beats her fists on the altar, is ironically misinterpreted by the saints as devout supplication. Florence has no faith that God can or does change a person's heart, including those of her brother and herself: "I done heard it said often enough, but I got yet to see it" (180). Years ago she revealed a hint of a belief in God's compassion in telling Elizabeth, "The Lord, he ain't going to let you fall so low" (182). After John emerges from his trial she shows him a rare gentleness due to her sense of satisfaction that he at least has wrested his birthright from the same man who took hers. But the letter she has carried for thirty years, with which she now threatens to destroy Gabriel, is a visible symbol of the hatred that has wasted her in the form of cancer. Florence's concluding remarks to Gabriel offer no reconciliation or forgiveness, only hatred and acrid threats of vengeance that fail to mask her defeat.

Gabriel's youthful carnality illustrates the dangers inherent in the church's negative attitude toward sexuality and secularity generally. Baldwin maintains the responsibility of individuals for their choices and actions; he also demonstrates how the church's strictures can stifle normal maturation and/or create an obsessive concern with sexual satisfaction. Although Elisha, a model of virtue and proper deportment, has been saved, he is forbidden the wholesome social development possible through dating because of the pastor's certain knowledge that "they would surely sin a sin beyond all forgiveness" (17). After being publicly admonished and humiliated in church for keeping company with a girl, Elisha boasts of successfully repressing his sexual urges, but Baldwin suggests the diminishment of a life in which, as Elisha says proudly, "You don't find no pleasure in the world" (54). Gabriel and John share the experience of teenage revolt against a parent's confining religion. But in contrast to John's earnest desire to learn about the world, Gabriel's early life of drunkenness and sensuality was truly depraved because he sought not enlightenment but only sensation. After his conversion and in his early preaching career, Gabriel's profound sense of his own sin was subsumed by and dissipated in his favorite theme of universal depravity. He displays the common tendency of the reformed to obsess on their former failings, finding them in everyone else, and associating any secular activity or interest with evil. Although his affair with Esther is only one among many of his sins, including more damaging offenses of omission such as abandoning Esther and Royal to their deaths and breaking his promise to be a real father to John, Gabriel fixates on it because of its sexual nature, and fails to recognize the pain and injury he has caused, and causes, many people. Despite his claim of divine direction, he chose both his wives out of a neurotic need for a perceived moral inferior and a morbid fascination with and lust for a "fallen woman." True to the church's dichotomous teaching, after Esther's death he finds popular music a reminder of his guilt, "not the music of the saints but another music, infernal, which glorified lust and held righteousness up to scorn" (136). When Gabriel met John as a baby, he interpreted John's attraction to blues music as a foreshadowing and symbol of his profane tendencies, condemning John in his heart (even before he knew of his illegitimacy) as evidence that "the Devil's working every day" (184).

Gabriel's theology, although partially an inheritance from his mother, is primarily a product of his own fear, egoism, and need to justify his own mean spirit. The God who suffered Gabriel's desperate youth hardens his heart to the sinner and cruelly waits to see him "cut down and banished" (96). In the depths of his sin, Gabriel thought "he had turned aside in sin too long, and God would not hear him" (97). Yet, at the moment of his conversion, his mother's imagined singing interceded for him, softening his heart and possibly that of the Lord, if only momentarily. His mother's absolute trust in God's promises, vindicated when she was freed from slavery after the war, extended to her belief that Gabriel would be saved. But the presumption of her latter conviction is paralleled in her son's habit of inventing promises and signs and ascribing them to God. In contrast to most of the other characters, whose certainty of falling to perdition fills their lives with an awful sense of doom, Gabriel enjoys the comfort of predestined greatness in the service of the Lord and the promise of a royal line of sons to carry on his work. Or so he decided, after mistaking his delusional fantasy of divine preferment in a dream for God's word and will. Gabriel's primary motive for seeking salvation was not holiness or service, but power and authority over others, suggesting his envy of God's mastery and his desire to be a little god. His judgment of the elders in the church shortly after his conversion reveals a brazen pride that only intensified with time. When he met Elizabeth and John, Gabriel determined that God had sent them as a sign of forgiveness for his destruction of Esther and Royal. Still, he has stood in judgment over Elizabeth for her supposed sins of loving Richard and giving birth to John, at first masking his denunciation under the condescending offer of help to "keep your foot from stumbling . . . again" (187). In his effort to deny responsibility for Roy's wild ways and likely doom, he relies on his fabrication of God's sign of approval and determines that "this living son, this headlong, living Royal might be cursed for the sin of his mother" (114) but certainly not for that of his father.

Humiliated by his poverty and his negligible status in the church, embittered by racism, and still driven by guilt over the sins of his past, Gabriel finds justification for "his daily anger . . . transformed into prophetic wrath" (15) in the church's image of God. Disturbed that John applies the Christian ideal of universal love even to white people, Gabriel attempts to convert John away from it by infusing into him Gabriel's racial hatred. When

Florence cries out to the Lord at the altar, Gabriel feels no compassion for the woman whose hand dared to stop him from beating his wounded son Roy; he feels only the desire for the Lord's vengeance as the instrument of his own reprisal, as he cries, "Have your way, Lord! Have your way!" (92). During John's nightlong struggle through spiritual darkness, Gabriel actually fears that he will be saved, and he hopes perversely that John will not see the Lord. When John finally is delivered, his father withholds all approval and encouragement and refuses to recognize John's "*new* name" (221) and spiritual identity, aware only of his own vastly diminished authority and capacity to terrorize the young man suddenly come of age.

Gabriel's history of delusive theology involves casting himself in biblical roles which minimize his culpability and warrant his abandonment of Royal and oppression of John. In Gabriel's two brilliant sermons presented in the novel, including the passionate, historic address inspired mostly by lust for Esther, he alludes to several biblical narratives that foreshadow his relationships with his sons Royal, Roy, and John. His basic theme of the failures of "many a father and mother who gave to their children not bread but a stone" (119) predicts the character of his paternity. His references in both sermons to the story of Cain's exile and loss of inheritance for killing his brother gain resonance in his present persecution of John. Gabriel takes the part of God in banishing the offender, but whereas God protects Cain, Gabriel wants John to remain as vulnerable as possible. Baldwin suggests that Gabriel somehow associates John's supposed sinfulness with the crime of Cain and that he sees John as the symbolic murderer of his illegitimate son Royal (and the potential symbolic murderer of Roy), exonerating Gabriel himself and requiring John's removal to prevent his usurping Royal's, and now Roy's birthright. In his dream Gabriel mistook the voice of his own ambition and vanity for that of God, making himself an Abraham chosen for exalted descendants. Allen points out that, in regarding Roy as his true heir, Gabriel links himself to Abraham (Allen, "Symbolism," 173), who exiled Ishmael, the son born of the slave Hagar, after God told him that He "would make a great nation of the slave-girl's son, too" (Genesis 21:13). Fearing John's potential greatness, Gabriel condemns him to emotional and psychological exile, as he did to Royal, who, like John, grew up "a stranger to his father and a stranger to God" (138). Just as Gabriel deemed Royal unworthy of acknowledgment and guidance, he also deems John unworthy of the love he promised. While John lies suffering and in peril on the threshing floor, Gabriel watches coldly as he reflects on the death by stabbing of his other disinherited son on a barroom floor.

Further biblical allusions parallel the conflicts between the father and his sons and heighten the sense of danger to John. Gabriel's first sermon dwelt on the pain of a father whose son goes astray and on the appalling sacrifice required of Abraham when he was ordered by God to kill Isaac, the son of God's promise finally fulfilled. In Gabriel's mind this theme tends to exculpate him for Royal's death, but in truth his bastard son was not sacrificed but thrown away in shame. Abraham offered up his beloved son, attaining in Kierkegaard's view the essence of faith, attainable not through certitude but only through believing despite ultimate risk and even impossibility: "Only he who descends to the underworld rescues the beloved, only he who draws the knife gets Isaac" (Kierkegaard 39). Gabriel makes no act of faith but treats God with contempt in his efforts to dispose of the despised fruits of sin, Royal and John, and he virtually attempts spiritual or psychic murder on God's altar.

John's reaction of disgust on seeing Gabriel naked not only suggests the inheritance of sexual repression and guilt but more importantly links John with Ham, whose viewing of his drunken, naked father earned him and his descendants Noah's curse that they would be slaves to their brothers. John sees the moral ugliness of Gabriel much more profoundly than Roy, whose utter resolve not to be saved prevents him from witnessing the depth of his father's deformity. John's most intense experience of his father's hypocrisy occurs in church as John lies beneath the minister of the Lord who is seeking to destroy his son's spirit. In his tribulation on the floor, John knows that, like Ham, he has been cursed by Gabriel for his knowledge, and he wonders whether Noah's curse, for generations used to justify the enslavement of blacks, could "come down so many ages"

(97) to afflict him. Although John, like Isaac's son Jacob, is not technically eligible for the birthright (Jacob because he was born a moment after Esau, John because he was born illegitimate), he struggles for its recognition and privilege. Esau's sale of his birthright to Jacob is analogous to Roy's rejection of the "holy" life, and Rebecca's favoring Jacob and scheming to win him Isaac's blessing corresponds to Elizabeth's special love for John and the secret signs with which she prepares him for his test. Although John's claim has a firmer basis than Jacob's and he does not employ trickery, like Jacob he knows that he risks bringing a further curse on himself instead of a blessing.

In his sermon before Esther, Gabriel also speaks of David and "his headlong son, Absalom" (119), who led a rebel army against his father, only to be killed by David's forces despite David's command of mercy. As with several of the biblical references, Gabriel prophesies his failures as a father and the consequent rebellions of his sons. But whereas David mourned openly for his dead son, saying, "I have no son to carry on my name" (II Samuel 18:18), for many years Gabriel stifles his sorrow over Royal's murder and the shame of his son's nameless birth. To Gabriel the story lends some justification for his abandonment of Royal and now John. Their revolts, like Absalom's against king and God, seemingly efface the requirement of a father's clemency. Although Gabriel excuses much in Roy, he deals severely with his youngest son's startling defiance, recognizing his own youthful willfulness resurrected and fearing that another son will repeat the fate of Absalom.

Although Elizabeth's early training impressed on her the same image of God which Gabriel learned, her refusal to live by the secular-sacred dichotomy has caused her considerable suffering yet also has prepared the way for John's crisis and opportunity. Her mother and aunt enforced a spiritless Christianity which rejected all traces of earthly pleasures, especially those her father made available running a "house." Elizabeth responded to and chose her father's warmth, gentleness, and love over the narrow, judgmental religion she was offered. Because Elizabeth was taught the dichotomy so indelibly when her father lost custody of her because of his disreputable occupation, she later believed she had to choose between Richard and God, between loving happiness and hollow rectitude. She believes that God caused Richard's death for the sin of their sexual union and because she conceived their child, and she now feels that God threatens her son because of her intransigence. Because she rightly refuses to believe that Richard's presence in her life was anything but sacred, Elizabeth waits in rising fear for God's final revenge, hoping that John "might be carried past wrath unspeakable, into a state of grace" (151) yet certain that "her prayers were in vain. What was coming would surely come; nothing could stop it" (175) because "there was no escape for anyone" (174). Just before John is about to curse God at the altar, Elizabeth reflects that she cursed God on the day of John's birth, an appropriate juxtaposition in that she has encouraged independent thinking and sown the seeds of rebellion in both her sons.

Elizabeth was heavily influenced by both her father's choice of the profane world and Richard's bitterness toward God, and she assumed the latter attitude to a greater degree after Richard's death. When she met Gabriel and accepted his attentions, she came to "embrace the faith she had abandoned" (186) as an insincere compromise for security for her son and herself. As John lies "astonished beneath the power of the Lord" (189), however, the prayers of Gabriel and Elizabeth signify their ironic reversal of roles and the dramatic conflict of their hopes for John. For while Gabriel fervently wishes that John will not emerge from the spiritual desert, Elizabeth prays to a God she has never known, in the face of certain impossibility, that He may relent in His vengeance and deliver her son. Elizabeth is like Hagar, whom Abraham sent into the wilderness with her son Ishmael and who feared his death when their water was finished, saying, "How can I watch the child die?" (Genesis 21:16). But God heard the child crying, showed Hagar where to find water for her son, and told her that He would make of him a great nation, as God does symbolically for Elizabeth and John. Elizabeth disguises her shock at John's salvation with quiet amazement and joy as she experiences her first moment of religious interiority in wonder at God's mercy. Her indirect but nonetheless powerful emotional communion with the Lord introduces Elizabeth to possibilities of authentic spiritual development which promise to recast her entire relationship with God. As she imagines Richard's voice on the morning of John's new life, she cries, knowing that the curse of loving Richard has been revoked and that the weakness which caused Richard's suicide has been eclipsed in John by other, restorative elements of his inheritance, both from Richard and from God.

Baldwin draws a clear contrast between individuals like Florence, Gabriel, and Elizabeth who rebel but still attempt to work within a restrictive theology, and antireligious characters whose guiltless secularity Baldwin sees as much healthier psychologically, and even close in some respects to the experience of the sacred. Elizabeth's father, Richard, and Esther – significantly, all from the past, and dead – were judged as sinful for their sexual acts or associations, yet each exercised an ability to love which transformed others. Elizabeth's father displayed the kind of "disreputable" behavior which Baldwin associates with Christ (RR 85), and Richard's blasphemous comment on Jesus, "You can tell that puking bastard to kiss my big black ass" (163), reflects Baldwin's wish to dethrone the false God (whether white or not) and replace him with the real one. Despite Gabriel's projections, there is no evidence that Esther was sexually promiscuous. Although she resolved to avoid holy men and the church after their affair, Esther preserved a sense of God which made her ashamed of being used. Royal and now Roy put themselves in jeopardy by flouting acceptably virtuous behavior, yet their rebellion against a warped religious perspective is, like others of this pattern, a necessary prelude to any possible exploration of true spirituality.

III

John's theology, based on the church's image of the terrible God, suffers from the redoubling force of Gabriel's severity and judgment. John feels that the church's rigid requirements for sanctity allow no room for real life, and he dreads the inevitable fate of "life awaiting him" (18) among the saved. His strenuous resistance to salvation, however, proceeds mostly from his decision not to "be like his father, or his father's fathers" (19), and his "heart was hardened against the Lord" (21) because bowing to God would entail capitulation to Gabriel. John therefore resists God's power in self-defense, scorning the saints of the Temple of the Fire Baptized and even doubting the existence of this God: "And why did they come here, night after night after night, calling out to a God who cared nothing for them – if, above this flaking ceiling, there was any God at all?" (81). Yet in spite of himself John has some form of belief in God, induced by both the "terror" and "wonder" (17) of the saints' rejoicing, which imparts to him an ineradicable sense of God's presence. Although at times John doubts God's capacity to change the troubled lives of those closest to him, at other times he desires the salvation whose power is evident on the transfigured face of Sister McCandless. Intuiting the travail he is about to undergo, John feels that God will force this suffering on him, but he also suspects that God may, by some unlikely chance, show him mercy and "the hand of God would reach down and raise him up" (145). John holds out the possibility of achieving sonship with his heavenly Father primarily to carry his quarrel with Gabriel "over his father's head to Heaven – to the Father who loved him" (145). John seeks an end to his hatred for his father, realizing that if he curses Gabriel on his deathbed Gabriel will become an "everlasting father" (146) – an inversion of the eternal Father as a source of love and peace – with the power even in the grave to thwart John's spiritual development.

The rebellious secularity John inherited from Elizabeth's father, from Elizabeth, and from his father Richard prepares him to resist the pseudo-religious repression of natural joys and to attempt to transcend the opposition between the secular and the sacred. John's healthy embrace of worldly interests and consolations was first evident in his gesture as a baby, on the day he met Gabriel, of extending his arms toward the blues music he heard, and dancing. The alternatives the church offers him comprise an awful, unacceptable either/or between immersion in sin and damnation and a sterile life without discovery, stimulation, or growth:

> John thought of Hell, of his soul's redemption, and struggled to find a compromise between the way that led to life everlasting and the way that ended in the pit. But there was none, for he had been raised in the truth. . . . Either he arose from this theater, never to return, putting behind him the world and its pleasures, its honors, and its glories, or he remained here with the wicked and partook of their certain punishment. (40)

The church's dichotomous thinking extends, at least in its minister Gabriel, to race relations. Baldwin hints of the church condoning hatred of whites in Gabriel's attitude that "all white people were wicked" (36), precisely the sentiment to which Baldwin objects in *The Fire Next Time* as evidence of the church as "a mask for hatred and self-hatred and despair" (FNT, 53). John, like Baldwin, takes very seriously the Christian injunction of universal love, and he recognizes that he will need God's help to avoid the self-destructive temptation of hating whites: "he feared them and knew that one day he could hate them if God did not change his heart" (37).

On John's fourteenth birthday, the day of his initiation into young manhood, his progressive resistance to Gabriel's bullying authority is carefully delineated, climaxing in John's near-curse of God. In the early scenes of the narrative John can "scarcely meet his father's eyes" (43), but by the time Elisha speaks from the church floor under the power of the Holy Spirit John stares at Gabriel in defiance, obeying the command to kneel but with "a movement like a curse" (150), reminding Gabriel of the many curses his victims have hurled at him. When John himself falls to the floor just at the moment he is to utter his blasphemy, he begins a journey of immense suffering through the infinity of psychic space between the hateful God and the source of love. The seemingly bottomless depth through which John continues to fall all night connotes his sense of sin as well as his despair that God's compassion is a myth. Separated utterly from all human support and love, feeling as though already in the grave,

John senses he will die if he does not find "something hidden in the darkness, that must be found" (199). His vision of Gabriel's violence and psychological brutality offer only a foretaste of John's eternal torment. Although John remains unaware that Gabriel is not his "real" father, he knows Gabriel has disinherited him, calling John in his reverie "the Devil's son" (198). As Ham, the disinherited son of Noah, John has witnessed his father's moral decrepitude: "I seen you under the robe, I seen you!" (199). As Ishmael, John feels exiled because his father has thrust him "out of the holy, the joyful, the blood-washed community" (196). At the climax of John's vision, Gabriel "raised his hand" and the "knife came down" (198), in a variation on the Abraham-Isaac account where obedient sacrifice becomes willful murder.

Baldwin depicts a variety of sources of succor that carry John through his experience of hell, including dependence on his own strength in the mythological quest for the father(s) (Lynch 157); his mother's intercessional prayer, sacrifice, and years of encouraging his independence; Elisha's brotherly, vigilant support; Richard's mysterious presence, conferring John's birthright; and God's love for His son. Amid the polyphony of significant voices heard, remembered, and imagined in the novel, one of the most crucial is the "malicious, ironic voice" insisting that John rise, "leave this temple and go out into the world" (193). Among the critical interpretations of this voice, the most convincing is Horace Porter's that it belongs to Richard (Porter 117), exhorting John to abandon the limitations of the world-hating religion of Gabriel and the church and to utilize the strengths and resources available to him as Richard's son: "Get up, John. Get up, boy. Don't let him keep you here. You got everything your daddy got" (196). John's unconscious knowledge of and communion with Richard enables him to call out, when Gabriel threatens him with the knife, "Father! Father!" (199), now almost able to believe in the heavenly Father because of the love of his dead father who never believed in God. After Elisha's voice encourages him to "go through" (202) and to call on God, John cries to the Lord directly for mercy. In the immediately following vision, John sees Gabriel and Elisha among a crowd of the saved who are revealed to be sinners with ragged robes "stained with unholy blood" (203) and struggling desperately toward the river of God's love and forgiveness. With this series of images John apprehends that even Elisha is a sinner and that even Gabriel, and John himself, deserve compassion.

The climax of John's night on the threshing floor, and of the novel, occurs in the next instant as John "goes through" and actually sees the Lord: "Then John saw the Lord – for a moment only; and the darkness, for a moment only, was filled with a light he could not bear. Then, in a moment, he was set free; his tears sprang as from a fountain; his heart, like a fountain of waters, burst" (204). Baldwin presents John's ecstatic experience of direct knowledge of God without irony, as John's "drifting soul was anchored in the love of God" (204). Baldwin emphasizes the vision as a glimpse of the hidden God, a momentary apparition such as a mystic might be granted with the potential to transform his life. John's moment stands between and is linked with Gabriel's epiphany of years ago when he discovered God's mercy, and Elizabeth's understated astonishment following John's deliverance.

The tenure of John's intimate association with his church may be, as Baldwin's was, somewhat limited because of the young man's resolve to live a full life and to transcend the church's contraposition of profane and holy joys. But the likely tenuousness of John's involvement in this community in no way diminishes the quality, significance, or perdurability of his new relationship with God, even though this God may remain, as in Baldwin's case, to a large extent unknown and perhaps unknowable. The Lord has turned aside Gabriel's attempts to disinherit, exile, and eliminate John, whose apparent defeat has been converted to startling victory. John has survived the curse on Ham and has even been rewarded for confronting Gabriel's moral deformity. The sins of the fathers, including Richard's instability and lack of faith in life, will not descend on John. He has returned from Ishmael's exile, saved by the river in his vision, as Ishmael was saved by the water God gave Hagar. Like Jacob, John has won his birthright, not just from the reluctant Gabriel but also from Richard and from God. Gabriel's hand with the raised knife has been stayed, and John rescued like Isaac from destruction. No longer a stranger to himself or to his fathers, John celebrates his first spiritual birthday as a son of God, who has written "his *new* name down in glory" (221) and who will sustain him in his struggles against sin and against Gabriel. John's greatest victory, however, is not over Gabriel but over his hatred of Gabriel, and his sincere smile at his temporal father, after briefly blocking his way into their home, indicates not just new strength but John's new freedom to love.

The theology of James Baldwin implicit in *Go Tell It on the Mountain* is firmly grounded in essential Christian belief with its treatment of motifs including death and resurrection, rebirth in a new identity, and the necessity for forgiveness. Baldwin also emphasizes much less common but by no means heretical themes of personal risk, objective uncertainty, and responsibility for saving others in the search for the Father. With his first novel Baldwin begins his analysis of the potential of suffering as a redemptive force if it is endured creatively (Nelson 121) and courageously. John Grimes becomes the prototype for many of Baldwin's protagonists in his suffering which leads himself and others to a greater understanding of themselves and God, and in his attempt to bridge the duality which unfortunately is promulgated by many Christians and which seeks to exclude much human experience from acceptable sources of spirituality. The concern with the potential of suffering for the transformation and sanctification of the individual and of others is central to Baldwin's spirituality. Hoyt Fuller notes that, according to Baldwin, the suffering caused by white racism has set African-Americans apart so that "they alone have retained a vision of a society constructed on the principles of justice and equality" (Fuller 327). This dubious blessing qualifies and positions the African-American as "the instrument of moral regeneration in American life," destined "at some indeterminate point in the future to be the salvation of this land, a task for which he is preeminently qualified by virtue of his prolonged stewardship in suffering" (Macebuh 121, 122). This theme, parallel to the messianic consciousness of nineteenth-century Russia as a "God-bearing people" (Gogol 51) called to save the West, is implicit in such pivotal works of African-American literature as Jean Toomer's *Cane* and Ralph Ellison's *Invisible Man* as well as in many of Baldwin's texts. Baldwin depicts the suffering of people of whatever color in order to concretize the idea of moral regeneration in the lives of a few individuals, suggesting hope for its realization on a much larger scale.

With John's survival and blessing by God, whereby "the love of God becomes . . . the cloak of manhood which is golden like the cross" (Allen, "Symbolism" 186), Baldwin not only explores the sacred but also insists on the potential sacredness of the secular. As demonstrated in the failures of Florence and Gabriel and in the victories of Elizabeth and John, for Baldwin authentic faith demands not only an open heart but also a dreadful risk and leap of trust toward a seemingly inscrutable God. Although Baldwin's theology exhibits a high degree of consistency, it evolves over the course of his career from fear to self-affirmation and from emphasis on the individual to the community. It develops more as a corrective to than a repudiation of Christian theology as understood and practiced, and might be called radical in the sense of being faithful to the spirit of the early church. Baldwin's whole career is a meditation on the meaning of conversion, as he frequently features the irony of the "religious" person converted away from religion. In essays, drama, and fiction he examines his own and his protagonists' crises of faith, their struggles which lead them away from the relatively shallow externality of dogma and certitude and toward greater interiority of uncertainty, subjectivity, risk, and love. From *Go Tell It on the Mountain* through his last work, *The Evidence of Things Not Seen*, he seeks but never seems to find and know the loving God, yet he repeatedly makes an act of faith in this unknown force. The title of his final novel, *Just Above My Head*, comes from a gospel song Ida Scott sings in *Another Country* and refers to this leap of faith in a God who is intuited but who always seems absent, removed: "Just above my head/ I hear music in the air/ And I really do believe/ There's a God somewhere."

Baldwin's theology considers three complementary aspects of salvation: saving oneself through developing the ability to survive and to love, saving another through preferential or erotic love, and saving others through selfless action based on accepting responsibility for all people. Although Baldwin's concept of salvation does not exclude (and even implies) a traditional Christian understanding of everlasting bliss, it also signifies survival and happiness in this world. The early works, *Go Tell It on the Mountain* and *The Amen Corner,* show salvation in the church as problematic and/or virtually impossible, and their focus shifts from damnation and the vengeful God to the individual's need to find sources of affirmation and grace outside the church – the individual must save himself or herself. As Baldwin expresses this thought explicitly, "You save yourself. If you have any sense at all and if you're lucky enough, you save yourself" (*Dialogue* 41). Although he wonders whether the Christian world has the requisite moral energy "to repent, to be born again," he finds hope in Christ's claim to be the Son of God "because it means that we are all the sons of God. . . . It is important to bear in mind that we are responsible for our soul's salvation. . . . Ultimately it is each man's responsibility alone" (*The Price of the Ticket,* hereafter PT, 441). As John Grimes achieves young manhood, he confronts the threat of the effacement of his personality by his father, his environment, and the church, and he risks psychic disintegration when he revolts against God. Although his temporary religious and psychological salvation is attributed by Baldwin partly to Christian faith and the loving Father, John's survival is achieved also by his own strength and his fidelity to the demands of the mythological quest for the father. John illustrates Baldwin's threefold thesis of salvation first, by depending on his own resources for spiritual growth; second, by receiving assistance and strength from Elisha, an implied and potential beloved; and third, by affecting his community now with his new vitality and confidence and realizing in the future his potential to save others as an artist. By undergoing the transformation required by faith, in Baldwin's view one comes to accept responsibility even for God: "One can begin to expand and transform God's nature, which has to be forever an act of creation on the part of every human being" (PT 441).

In the introduction to *The Price of the Ticket,* written two years before Baldwin's death, he admits he may never have abandoned his "obsession" with religion: "If I were still in the pulpit which some people (and they may be right) claim I never left, I would counsel my countrymen to the self-confrontation of prayer, the cleansing breaking of the heart which precedes atonement" (PT xviii). Although he says that "in order to become a moral human being" he may have to "stay out of the temple" (RR 86), a phrase echoing the advice of the voice of Richard to John in *Go Tell It on the Mountain,* Baldwin's investment in Christian spirituality remains extensive though often subtle as he openly "questions divine existence while still courting its allegiance" (O'Neale 140). In spite of the significance to Baldwin's works of the spiritual dialectic of revolt and faith, the latter element has received very little critical attention. In contrast to many scholars who find in Baldwin predominant and progressive negativity and decline, as well as disinterest in Christian theology, O'Neale claims that "the unfailing optimism seen in the entirety of his work, that only love within and between the races will ultimately save America . . . is rooted in the philosophy of Christian faith" (O'Neale 131). She adeptly identifies the hiddenness of his faith and also suggests his motive in withholding an overt declaration:

> Baldwin still attempts to separate the visible history of black America's experience with Christianity from the spiritual, visionary experience that both he and the race may have internalized. The reality of that unseen truth . . . enables him to keep advocating that the demonstrable love of Christ will bring to earth that paradise revealed on the threshing floor. . . . Then and only then will his quest end and he can unhesitantly acknowledge oneness with the Christian God, his father. Until that essence of true Christianity is revealed, Baldwin's dissociation from variant fathers tempts him to withhold absolute commitment. (O'Neale 141)

Although his commitment may necessarily be incomplete, Baldwin's dedication to the personal quest for the hidden God, fired by the glimpse he shares in *Go Tell It on the Mountain,* extends through *The Evidence of Things Not Seen.*

NOTES

1 The predominant majority of Baldwin scholars tend to view his work through the distorting lens of dichotomy, frequently dismissing much of his work for its alleged rage and obsession with narrow, temporal political matters. C. W. E. Bigsby, in a classic misreading of the second half of Baldwin's career, finds "a sullen determinism" (Bigsby 114), arguing that Baldwin's "early faith in the moral responsibility of the individual and the possibility of social change was destroyed" (Bigsby 115). Bigsby's privileging of social analysis reveals his own dichotomous mind and aligns him with other critics who have invented a naturalistic Baldwin out of one whose consistent impulse is to insist on human freedom and responsibility. Edward Margolies emphasizes Baldwin as merely one writer in the "generations of Negro polemicists" (Margolies 74), and he reduces Baldwin to a symbol of "the transfer of religious energies to political and social causes" (Margolies 60). Representative of the approach of many critics, Stanley Macebuh inaccurately regards even relatively early works such as *Another Country* as part of "a chronological spiral of rage" (Macebuh 46). Discussing most of Baldwin's output in confining sociological terms, he concludes that the works of the late 60s and early 70s represent a conversion to a "quintessential social fury" (Macebuh 35).

2 Of the five full-length studies of Baldwin's fiction and drama, only Macebuh's deals in any detail with his spirituality, offering the intriguing if exaggerated thesis that "theological terror" pervades Baldwin's work. Despite the implicit binarism of Macebuh's approach and the dissolution of his thesis in favor of a progressively politicized focus, he does at least establish the relevance of theology to Baldwin's vision. The only other book that touches on issues relating to Christianity is that of Trudier Harris, who perceptively discusses the deforming effects of the church on black women as it encourages their subservience to men and infuses them with guilt. But her analysis does not address Baldwin's theology except for a few brief observations. The reactions in almost all the articles to the religious theme range from ignoring or denying it to very brief mention and scant analysis.

3 Baldwin was much influenced in this respect by Wright's *Native Son* and by Dostoevsky's *Crime and Punishment*, *The Devils*, and *The Brothers Karamazov*.

WORKS CITED

Allen, Shirley S. "The Ironic Voice in Baldwin's *Go Tell It on the Mountain.*" In O'Daniel, pp. 30–37.

"Religious Symbolism and Psychic Reality in Baldwin's *Go Tell It on the Mountain.*" In Standley, *Critical Essays,* pp. 166–88.

Baldwin, James. *The Fire Next Time.* New York: Dial, 1963.

Go Tell It on the Mountain. New York: Dell, 1952.

The Price of the Ticket. New York: St. Martin's, 1985.

Baldwin, James, and Nikki Giovanni. *A Dialogue.* New York: J. P. Lippincott, 1973.

Baldwin, James, and Margaret Mead. *A Rap on Race.* New York: Dell, 1971.

Bigsby, C. W. E. "The Divided Mind of James Baldwin." In Bloom, pp. 113–29.

Bloom, Harold, ed. *James Baldwin.* New York: Chelsea House, 1986.

Fabre, Michel. "Fathers and Sons in James Baldwin's *Go Tell It on the Mountain.*" In Keneth Kinnamon, ed., *James Baldwin: A Collection of Critical Essays.* Englewood Cliffs, NJ: Prentice-Hall, 1974.

Fuller, Hoyt. "Contemporary Negro Fiction." *Southwest Review* 50 (Autumn 1965): 321–335.

Gibson, Donald B. "James Baldwin: The Political Anatomy of Space." In O'Daniel, pp. 3–18.

Gogol, Nikolai. *Selected Passages from Correspondence with Friends.* Trans. Jesse Zeldin. Nashville: Vanderbilt University Press, 1969.

Harris, Trudier. *Black Women in the Fiction of James Baldwin.* Knoxville: University of Tennessee Press, 1985.

Kierkegaard, Soren. *Fear and Trembling and The Sickness Unto Death.* Trans. Walter Lowrie. Princeton: Princeton University Press, 1954.

Lynch, Michael F. "The Everlasting Father: Mythic Quest and Rebellion in Baldwin's *Go Tell It on the Mountain.*" *CLA Journal* 37 (December 1993): 156–175.

Macebuh, Stanley. *James Baldwin.* New York: Third Press, 1973.

Margolies, Edward. "The Negro Church: James Baldwin and the Christian Vision." In Bloom, pp. 59–76.

Nelson, Emmanuel. "James Baldwin's Vision of Otherness and Community." In Standley, *Critical Essays,* pp. 121–124.

O'Daniel, Therman, ed. *James Baldwin: A Critical Evaluation.* Washington, D.C.: Howard University Press, 1977.

O'Neale, Sondra. "Fathers, Gods, and Religion: Perceptions of Christianity and Ethnic Faith in James Baldwin." In Standley, *Critical Essays,* pp. 125–143.

Porter, Horace A. *Stealing the Fire: The Art and Protest of James Baldwin.* Middletown, CT: Wesleyan University Press, 1989.

Scott, Nathan A., Jr. "Judgment Marked by a Cellar: The American Negro Writer and the Dialectic of Despair." In Harry J. Mooney, Jr. and Thomas F. Staley, eds., *The Shapeless God.* Pittsburgh: University of Pittsburgh Press, 1968, pp. 139–169.

Standley, Fred L. "*Go Tell It on the Mountain:* Religion as the Indirect Method of Indictment." In Standley, *Critical Essays,* pp. 188–194.

Standley, Fred L., and Nancy V. Burt, eds. *Critical Essays on James Baldwin.* Boston: G. K. Hall, 1988.

Warren, Nagueyalti. "The Substance of Things Hoped For: Faith in *Go Tell It on the Mountain.*" *Obsidian II* 7 (Spring–Summer 1992): 19–32.

3

The South in *Go Tell It on the Mountain:* Baldwin's Personal Confrontation

HORACE PORTER

JAMES Baldwin's *Go Tell It on the Mountain* has been appropriately designated an autobiographical or semiautobiographical work. I have previously tried to suggest how it would be useful to read the novel with a more comprehensive definition of autobiography in mind.[1] I concluded:

> One could persuasively read passages [from his stories and novels] as fictional counterparts of Baldwin's comments in *Notes of a Native Son,* in *The Devil Finds Work,* and in other autobiographical essays. But this direct referential approach, in which the "facts" of John Grimes's life are correctly perceived as mirroring Baldwin's, amounts to only a useful interpretive beginning, not a critical end. The point of view from which one scrutinizes the facts of a writer's life as a writer is also crucial. Thus, the literal facts of Baldwin's boyhood . . . pale in significance beside the "secrets" of his literary life embedded in the text of *Go Tell It on the Mountain.*[2]

A writer writes a novel at a particular time in a specific place and at a certain moment in her or his career. Such significant factors, in addition to the fidelity of the plot and characters to the biographical details of a writer's life, are important considerations. For instance, *Go Tell It on the Mountain* is Baldwin's first novel rather than his sixth. That fact is at least as important as the similarity between Gabriel Grimes, John Grimes's dogmatic and bitter stepfather, and David Baldwin, Baldwin's own stepfather.

Consequently, I refer to *Go Tell It on the Mountain* as a "proving ground" to underscore its weighty psychological and emotional significance in Baldwin's literary career. The "autobiography" that seems of crucial significance is the story of the writer's attempt to achieve a coherent evocation of a difficult subject no less than an initial realization of his talent.

The challenge Baldwin faced partly involved the portrayal of Gabriel Grimes, a bitter black Southerner who had, like his own stepfather, come north to New York. Having never even visited, let alone lived in the South, Baldwin, in writing his first novel was wholly dependent on vicarious experience – reading, observation, and imagination – in his portrayal of Gabriel Grimes's complex and bewildering fate. We should bear in mind, as previously noted by various critics and Baldwin himself, that the gestation period of *Go Tell It on the Mountain* was long and painful. Responding to Wolfgang Binder in an interview conducted in 1980, Baldwin commented:

> I finished my first novel, *Go Tell It on the Mountain* . . . and it was a turning point in my life, because it proved to me, not so much to the world but to me and my baby sister that at least I was serious. A black writer in the world that I had grown up in was not so much wicked, he was insane. So when *Mountain* finally came out in 1953, at least I had proved something to people. And then the real battle began. But nothing happened to me afterwards that was quite as terrifying as the very beginning. I knew that if I could not finish *Mountain* I would never be able to finish anything after that. But that was my ticket to something else. I finally had gotten it. At least I was a writer.[3]

The autobiographical fact that is of primary interest has less to do with the terrifying presence of David Baldwin and Gabriel Grimes in the lives of their respective sons as Baldwin's "terrifying" beginning as a writer.

Furthermore, long before a series of biographical works began to appear shortly after the writer's death, Baldwin had become (partly through his own eloquent autobiography) legendary. His was a literary Cinderella story involving his flight from the Harlem ghetto to Paris, London, Hollywood, Istanbul, and St. Paul de Vence. He became a best-selling author. He was invited to the White House by President John Kennedy. And after the publication of *The Fire Next Time* in 1963, he was featured on the cover of *Time*. Excluding Baldwin's final years when he lived and taught in the United States (calling himself a "commuter") he spent most of his writing life in France – Paris and St. Paul de Vence.

After his initial long stay in Paris (1948–1957), Baldwin returned to the United States. He spent a few weeks at home with his family in New York and then headed south for the first time. He had been commissioned by *Harper's Magazine* and *Partisan Review* to write essays on the various strategies and programs for bringing an end to racial discrimination and separation. For a month or so during September and October of 1957, Baldwin traveled through a number of southern cities – Charlotte, Atlanta, Birmingham, Montgomery, and Tuskegee. During his stay in Atlanta, he met and interviewed Dr. Martin Luther King, Jr. And while in Birmingham, he met with Rev. Fred Shuttlesworth, a stalwart leader and defender of the rights of African-Americans.[4]

After his return to New York, Baldwin wrote two essays – "The Hard Kind of Courage" which was published in *Harper's Magazine* and would be included in his second collection of essays, *Nobody Knows My Name* (1961) as "A Fly in the Buttermilk." He called the essay he wrote for *Partisan Review* "A Letter From the South: Nobody Knows My Name." It became the title piece of the writer's second volume of essays. These eloquent articles reveal the writer's complex attitudes toward the South. They were also clearly designed to educate, provoke, and inspire a liberal white audience, to awaken the audience from its slumber of moral denial and evasiveness on racial discrimination. In this regard, the essays are a rehearsal for *The Fire Next Time*, his most famous essay, which appeared in its original form in *The New Yorker*.

Thus, Baldwin could neither get around the demands of his own literary design, his conscious and unconscious professional or vocational desire, nor could he avoid entirely a temporary form of blinding northern and cosmopolitan prejudice. He was victimized partly by the mythology of the South. He viewed the South rather reductively as a slow, backward, and brutal land, trapped perpetually in the nightmare of its racial history. In "Nobody Knows My Name" he recalls his thoughts as his plane landed in the South for the first time:

[M]y plane hovered over the rust-red earth of Georgia. I was past thirty, and I had never seen this land before. I pressed my face against the window, watching the earth come closer; soon we were just above the tops of the trees. I could not suppress the thought that this earth had acquired its color from the blood that had dripped down from these trees. My mind now filled with the image of a black man, younger than I, perhaps, or my own age, hanging from a tree, while white men watched him and cut his sex from him with a knife.[5]

Baldwin concludes, directly after the preceding passage: "My father must have seen such sights – he was very old when he died – or heard of them, or had this danger touch him."[6] This quotation demonstrates how preoccupied Baldwin was with a sense of the South's emasculating, murderous, and bloody past, a picture of the region paradoxically as mythological as it was real.

Almost two decades after the publication of *Go Tell It on the Mountain,* Baldwin, the most famous African-American writer alive at that time, published *No Name in the Street* (1972), recalling images of the South highly similar to those passing through his mind as his plane landed for the first time:

There was more than enough to fascinate. In the Deep South – Florida, Georgia, Alabama, Mississippi, for example – there is the great, vast, brooding, welcoming, and bloodstained land, beautiful enough to astonish and break the heart. The land seems nearly to weep beneath the burden of this civilization's unnamable excrescences. The people and the children wander blindly through the forest of billboards, antennae, Coca-Cola bottles, gas stations, drive-ins, motels, beer cans, music of a strident and invincible melancholy, stilted wooden porches, snapping fans, aggressively blue-jeaned buttocks, strutting crotches, pint bottles, condoms, in the weeds, rotting automobile corpses, brown as beetles, earrings flashing in the gloom of bus stops: over all there seems to hang a miasma of lust and longing and rage. Every southern city seemed to me to have been but lately rescued from the swamps, which were patiently waiting to reclaim it. The people all seemed to remember their time under water, and to be both dreading and anticipating their return to that freedom from responsibility. Every black man, whatever, his style, had been scarred, as in some tribal rite; and every white man, though white men, mostly, had no style, had been maimed. And, everywhere, the women, the most fearfully mistreated creatures of this region, with narrowed eyes and pursed lips – lips turned inward on a foul aftertaste – watched and rocked and waited.[7]

The preceding passage, marked at once by the best and worst of Baldwin's imagination, captures a certain mythological sense of the South. Baldwin uses a hard-edged documentary style: "billboards, antennae, Coca-Cola bottles, gas stations, drive-ins, motels, beer cans." This Whitmanian catalogue of images is presented fleetingly as though a montage viewed rapidly from the window of a moving automobile. And while he speaks of "the Deep South" as a land "beautiful enough to astonish and break the heart" he squeezes "Florida, Georgia, Alabama, Mississippi" together as monolithic "bloodstained land."

To be sure, he succeeds at evoking a physical sense of the southern scene. There are indeed "rotting automobile corpses, brown as beetles," all over the South. But some may also be rotting in New Jersey and New York. What is more significant is the obvious outsider's contempt Baldwin displays. His contempt is betrayed by his dispassionate bitterness. "The land," as he labels it in a superior tone, is vastly removed from New York, let alone Paris, his beloved city of light. "The land," which is "the Deep South" "seems nearly to weep beneath the burden of this civilization's unnamable excrescences." This image of the South haunts Baldwin and is a recurrent theme in his work. It is hardly accidental that Baldwin's initial thought of the South as his plane landed is a vivid scene of lynching, a deeply internalized and bloody scene of castration and death.

He knows that "this land" inspired his stepfather's lifelong hatred of whites. Thus, his sense of the place terrorizes him even as he arrives. Shortly thereafter, as though the gods had arranged a ritualistic scene of initiation and instruction, Baldwin walked through the front door of a cafeteria in Montgomery. It was as though he had stumbled back in time to a revelatory moment that explained what his stepfather had so painfully endured.

The writer captures this memorable incident in *No Name in the Street:*

> I will never forget it, I don't know if I can describe it. Everything abruptly froze into what, even at that moment, struck me as a kind of

Marx Brothers parody of horror. Every white face turned to stone: the arrival of the messenger of death could not have had a more devastating effect than the appearance in the restaurant doorway of a small, unarmed, utterly astounded black man. I had realized my error as soon as I opened the door: but the absolute terror on all these white faces – I swear that not a soul moved – paralyzed me. They stared at me, I stared at them.[8]

When he is "barked" at by a waitress who yells "What you want boy? What you want in here?" Baldwin backs out. A white man suddenly appears and advises him to go to the back: "Right around there, boy. Right around there." When Baldwin arrives at the "colored entrance," he concludes: "And this was a dreadful moment – as brief as lightning and far more illuminating. I realized that this man thought that he was being kind, and he was, indeed, being as kind as expected from a guide in hell."[9]

After Baldwin goes through the "colored entrance" and orders a hamburger, he highly respects the blacks who have been able to adjust and adapt to the southern situation while still maintaining their dignity. He considered himself incapable of such patience and forbearance. As he watched a black man eat a hamburger in apparent aimless abandon, he concluded: "I was far from certain that I was equipped to get through a single day down here. . . . They had been undergoing and overcoming for a very long time without me . . . my role was to do a story and avoid becoming one. I watched the patient man as he ate, watched him with both wonder and respect."[10]

As previously noted, during the period that Baldwin spent writing *Go Tell It on the Mountain,* he had not yet gone to the "old country," as he calls it. Thus, he was entirely at the mercy of his imagination, reading, and whatever conclusions he drew about the region based on the limitations and strengths – real and imagined – of his stepfather's personality. This autobiographical situation partly explains the writer's portrait of Gabriel Grimes, no less than John's response to him in the novel.

Two themes inextricably linked in *Go Tell It on the Mountain* involve the perpetual existence of black rage and the manner in which such rage can either be self-destructive or transformative. These two themes are connected to the image of the South in *Go*

Tell It on the Mountain because, as Baldwin sees it, the incipient black rage is partly the legacy of the South playing itself out in the individual as well as collective lives of blacks in the North. For instance, Elizabeth and Richard, John Grimes's biological parents, flee the South in order to marry and fulfill their dreams in the North. Richard eventually commits suicide, leaving Elizabeth with John and the memory of his love and self-destructive bitterness.

Baldwin explores the sources and consequences of such complex emotional dynamics in *Go Tell It on the Mountain.* And precisely because he was able to begin fulfilling his own dream of becoming a writer by completing his first novel he was later able to clarify and name in "Notes of a Native Son" the rage and avenging will he felt in his teens and early twenties.

A telling moment of truth arises in *Notes of a Native Son* when Baldwin's father asks him whether he would rather write or preach. The memory of, or indeed remembering, this incident is an inspired moment. As the minister delivers the eulogy at his father's funeral Baldwin, having celebrated his nineteenth birthday earlier that day, unexpectedly remembers the singular incident: "I remembered the one time in all our life together when we had really spoken to each other. It was on a Sunday and it must have been shortly before I left home. We were walking, just the two of us, in our usual silence, to or from church. I was in high school and had been doing a lot of writing and I was, at about this time, the editor of the high school magazine. But I had also been a young minister and had been preaching from the pulpit. . . . my father asked me abruptly, 'you'd rather write than preach, wouldn't you?' That was all we said. It was awful to remember that that was all we had *ever* said."[11]

This passage represents a highly revelatory autobiographical moment whether one considers it in light of *Notes of a Native Son* or in relation to *Go Tell It on the Mountain.* When Baldwin says he would rather write than preach, he is asserting so much more than the straightforward statement apparently indicates. The statement takes us considerably beyond a mere choice of vocation. Writing represents a comprehensive way of seeing and a habit of being in the world.

To write or preach is the figurative question on Baldwin's mind as he creates John Grimes and his brooding stepfather, the Reverend Gabriel Grimes, in *Go Tell It on the Mountain*. The opening paragraph of the novel, no less than Part One, "The Seventh Day," addresses the matter of John Grimes's potential fate relative to that of his stepfather: "Everyone had always said that John would be a preacher when he grew up, just like his father. It had been said so often that John, without ever thinking about it, had come to believe it himself. Not until the morning of his fourteenth birthday did he really begin to think about it, and by then it was too late."[12]

The opening lines of the novel suggest the literal and figurative weight of paternal authority in the work. The narrator also foregrounds the issue in an implicitly antagonistic or indeed oedipal way: "Not until the morning of his fourteenth birthday did he really begin to think about it and by then it was too late." The passage clearly suggests John's apparent, if adolescent, ambivalence about life as a minister. And as the first section of the novel develops, we discover that John finds the attractions outside the church equally and perhaps even more alluring. The narrator alludes to John's sense of "the darkness of his father's house."[13]

Furthermore, we learn that John's response to the assertion that one day he would be a "Great Leader of His People" is negative and defiant: "John was not much interested in his people and still less in leading them anywhere."[14] John has dreams of another kind of public role. He envisions himself as "a poet, or college president, or a movie star; he drank expensive whiskey, and he smoked Lucky Strike cigarettes in the green package."[15]

Baldwin takes considerable care in the novel's opening section to provide the reader with a sharply sketched portrait of John. We know, for instance, that he is singularly intelligent. And given his precocious nature, he discovers that he can use his intelligence as a source of pride and protection. He makes this discovery when a principal singles him out in the first grade. She refers to him as "a very bright boy" after noticing work with the alphabet that he had done at the blackboard. This moment of recognition becomes a scene of extraordinary empowerment: "That moment gave him from that time on, if not a weapon at least a shield; he apprehended totally, without belief or understanding, that he had in himself a power that other people lacked; that he could use this to save himself, to raise himself; and that, perhaps, with this power he might one day win that love which he so longed for."[16]

John's yearning for power is expressed most dramatically in the passage often quoted in which he stands on top of a hill in Central Park and imagines his future as a "giant" or "tyrant":

> At a point that he knew by instinct and by the shape of the buildings surrounding the park, he struck out on a steep path over-grown with trees, and climbed a short distance until he reached the clearing that led to the hill. Before him, then, the slope stretched upward, and above it the brilliant sky, and beyond it, cloudy, and far away, he saw the skyline of New York. He did not know why, but there arose in him an exultation and a sense of power, and he ran up the hill like an engine, or a madman, willing to throw himself headlong into the city that glowed before him.
>
> But when he reached the summit he paused; he stood on the crest of the hill, hands clasped beneath his chin, looking down. Then he, John, felt like a giant who might crumble this city with his anger; he felt like a tyrant who might crush this city beneath his heel; he felt like a long-awaited conqueror at whose feet flowers would be strewn, and before whom multitudes cried, Hosanna! He would be, of all, the mightiest, the most beloved, the Lord's anointed; and he would live in this shining city which his ancestors had seen with longing from far away. For it was his; the inhabitants of the city had told him it was his; he had but to run down, crying, and they would take him to their hearts and show him wonders his eyes had never seen.[17]

Since John Grimes knows the point in Central Park "by instinct" and since he "struck out" for it, Baldwin suggests that John's is a recurrent fantasy that he is driven to act out. "He did not know why, but there arose in him an exultation and a sense of power, and he ran up the hill like an engine, or a madman." The setting, Central Park, is a noted public space in America's largest and most influential city. Thus, John's fantasy also betrays genuine ambition and a personality marked by a need for consummate self-expression. John's adolescent self gives way to a raging spirit within him, which the narrator likens to that of a "madman," but the metaphorical resonance of the passage does not suggest madness so much as profoundly troubling ambivalence. John's adolescent fantasy is symptomatic of his struggle with "the darkness of his father's house" and "Jesus in the darkness of his father's church" but it also represents Baldwin's early and figurative meditation on his complex and bewildering fate as an artist. The immediate scene is superimposed on a more significant aspect almost hidden in John's avenging imagination, the portrait of an ambitious young artist with a confident and raging will to public expression and power.[18]

Even here where the South has no ostensible relation to the moment, there are significant connections. The Manhattan skyline represents the antithesis of his father's house. Gabriel Grimes has brought the emotional baggage of the South north with him. It is this legacy that threatens to limit John's possibilities.

Furthermore, Gabriel Grimes is a man victimized and burdened by the sins of his past. The South – "the blood stained land" – is the scene of his personal fall from the glory of God as well as the space in which his embattled black manhood has been so ruthlessly socialized. Thus, his rage, his hatred, suspicion, and contempt for whites periodically erupt. The "rage in his blood," to borrow from Baldwin's *Notes of a Native Son,* is essentially a southern rage. And it is this rage that is literally John Grimes's legacy, the nightmarish history with which he must contend and which he must overcome.

Consequently, it is hardly an accident that a bloody image of a murdered and castrated black man should also appear in *Go Tell It on the Mountain* and that such a moment would directly involve Gabriel Grimes. The moment comes in "Gabriel's Prayer" as the Reverend worries about his favorite son Royal. As he walks through town threatened by the hostility of the white men who watch him, he muses:

> There were no black men on the streets at all, save him. There had been found that morning, just outside of town, the dead body of a soldier, his

uniform shredded where he had been flogged, and, turned upward through the black skin, raw, red meat. He lay face downward at the base of a tree, his fingernails digging into the scuffed earth. When he was turned over, his eyeballs stared upward in amazement and horror, his mouth was locked open wide; his trousers, soaked with blood, were torn open, and exposed to the cold, white air of morning the thick hairs of his groin, matted together, black and rust-red, and the wound that seemed to be throbbing still. He had been carried home in silence and lay now behind locked doors, with his living kinsmen, who sat, weeping, and praying, and dreaming of vengeance, and waiting for the next visitation. Now, someone spat on the sidewalk at Gabriel's feet, and he walked on, his face not changing, and he heard it reprovingly whispered behind him that he was a good nigger, surely up to no trouble.[19]

The recurrent image of a lynched black man in Baldwin's work is a telling detail. In *Go Tell It on the Mountain*, the castrated and dead body of the black man simultaneously signifies powerlessness and avenging rage. In many instances black men were lynched on the basis of mere suspicion and false claims about their sexual involvement with white women. They found themselves trapped in a web of psycho-sexual circumstances which often led to death. Their legacy was the anger of their bereaved kin – fathers and mothers, sisters and brothers. It is no wonder that directly after Gabriel Grimes merely hears about the dead black soldier, he responds vicariously in a deep psychological and visceral way. He is surrounded by white men watching him in a threatening manner: "While he walked, held by his caution more rigid than an arrow, he prayed, as his mother had taught him to pray, for loving kindness; yet he dreamed of the feel of a white man's forehead against his shoe; again and again, until the head wobbled on the broken neck and his foot encountered nothing but the rushing blood."[20] It is significant to note here, however, that the preceding scene does not involve so much a ritual as a horrible *fait accompli*. The man had already been killed and castrated, leaving "the wound that seemed to be throbbing still."[21] Furthermore, the scene shows Gabriel Grimes worrying about the apple of his eye, his son Royal, whom he briefly encounters and warns to be careful.

The figure of the lynched black man who first appears in

Baldwin's fiction in *Go Tell It on the Mountain* surfaces again in *Nobody Knows My Name* and is fully explored in *Going to Meet the Man.* Here is the lynching scene from that story.

The man with the knife walked toward the crowd, smiling slightly; as though this were a signal, silence fell, he heard his mother cough. Then the man with the knife walked up to the hanging body. He turned and smiled again. Now there was a silence all over the field. The hanging head looked up. It seemed fully conscious now, as though the fire had burned out terror and pain. The man with the knife took the nigger's privates in his hand, one hand, still smiling, as though he were weighing them. In the cradle of the one white hand, the nigger's privates seemed as remote as meat being weighed in the scales; but seemed heavier, too, much heavier, and Jesse felt his scrotum tighten; and huge, huge, much bigger than his father's, flaccid, hairless, the largest thing he had ever seen till then, and the blackest. The white hand stretched them, cradled them, caressed them. Then the dying man's eyes looked straight into Jesse's eyes – it could not have been as long as a second, but it seemed longer than a year. Then Jesse screamed, and the crowd screamed as the knife flashed, first up, then down, cutting the dreadful thing away, and the blood came roaring down.[22]

This bloody image partly represents Baldwin's ongoing effort to make articulate the significance and consequences of his stepfather's life in his own. It represents a memory of the South apparently deep-seated in a region of his mind.

In *Exorcising Blackness: Historical and Literary Lynching and Burning Rituals,* Trudier Harris provides a heart-wrenching picture of the lynching ritual. She describes how it encapsulates for the white onlookers – men, women, and children – elements of theater of the grotesque, sport, and entertainment.[23]

I referred earlier to Baldwin's sense of the South on his first visit there in 1957 as being paradoxically as mythological as it was real. Apparently, this sense of the South persisted. In *Going to Meet the Man* (1965), Baldwin provides a *tableau vivant* of the lynching ritual from its start to its bloody end. David Leeming has commented that Baldwin (during 1965) wrote the story "more easily, he said, than he had written anything."[24] Leeming sums up the significance of the story in the following manner:

The story "Going to Meet the Man" was a fictional articulation of ideas that its author had also treated in his essays; like all of Baldwin's fiction, it can best be seen as a parable, in this case a parable on the relationship between racism and sexuality, in which the white sheriff, from whose point of view the story of a lynching is told, becomes a representative of the long-held Baldwin belief that the race problem – the so-called Negro problem – was really a white problem. The "man" in "Going to Meet the Man" is the white man, as was "Mister Charlie" in *Blues for Mister Charlie.* The black man who is lynched during the sheriff's childhood is, like so many earlier fictional creations of Baldwin's mind, a scapegoat for the facing of the race problem. Hanging on the tree, deprived of his masculinity in a violent ritual of castration rooted in the white man's myth of black sexuality, he provides the white man – represented by the sheriff – with the sexual power he otherwise lacks.

We can speculate and extrapolate and use some of Baldwin's own words ("My father must have seen such sights . . . or heard of them, or had this danger touch him") in order to conclude that Baldwin's stepfather actually told the young writer such horror stories about the South. We certainly know that David Baldwin was extremely suspicious of, and disapproved of Baldwin's association with, whites on the grounds that they could not be trusted. However, to whatever degree the horror of the South lived on in Baldwin's mind – as demonstrated over time by his stories and essays – the direct autobiographical influence of his father through tales of southern lynchings is finally less significant than the comprehensive and indirect threat the South posed to his literary ambition.

David Baldwin's bitter perspective on the world, no less than his embattled pride and sense of manly dignity, is what he tried, with patriarchal authority and studied vengeance, to pass on to his young stepson. And in his instinctive, inchoate writer's way Baldwin, like John Grimes, began to covet and protect his intelligence, his developing literary sensibility, as a barrier of protection between him and the stepfather he feared. This particular oedipal dynamic leads him to tell his stepfather one fateful Sunday morning that he would rather write than preach.

The various lynching scenes highlighting Baldwin's preoccupation with images of powerlessness and emasculation, the ultimate rooting out of manhood and authority, along with John Grimes's dreams of a world beyond "the darkness of his father's house" surface repeatedly. We have already discussed his fantasy on the hill in Central Park. A similar moment and perhaps of equal significance occurs when he travels defiantly downtown and watches a movie alone. The movie is set in London.

The image of a woman John Grimes sees in a movie becomes an appropriate metonym of his rage, defiance, and artistic desire. I readily concede that any direct connection to John Grimes's (read James Baldwin's) views about the South is not readily apparent. But here I return to my initial suggestion of a more comprehensive and perhaps more significant definition of autobiography. The woman appears as a fleeting image on the silver screen as John Grimes's mind is wavering to and fro between the pleasure this dark and forbidden (by Gabriel Grimes) palace of illusion affords his inchoate artistic or literary sensibility and the intense anguish it inspires about the damnation that awaits him for his defiance and sinful indulgence.

Against Gabriel Grimes's expressed wishes, John finds himself wandering down 42nd Street past "the stone lions that guarded the great main building of the Public Library, a building filled with books and unimaginably vast."[25] He imagines a future life of glamour and power. He eventually finds himself in front of the movie houses. He enters one and watches a movie about a woman who lived in London: "She had a great many boyfriends, and she smoked cigarettes and drank."[26] John Grimes identifies with her for the following reasons:

> Nothing tamed or broke her, nothing touched her, neither kindness, nor scorn, nor hatred, nor love. She had never thought of prayer. It was unimaginable that she would ever bend her knees and come crawling along the dusty floor to anybody's altar, weeping for forgiveness. Perhaps her sin was so extreme that it could not be forgiven; perhaps her pride was so great that she did not need forgiveness. She had fallen from that high estate which God had intended for men and women, and she made her fall glorious because it was so complete. John could not have found in his heart, had he dared to search it any wish for her redemption. He wanted to be like her, only more powerful, more

thorough, and more cruel; to make those around him, all who hurt him, suffer as she made the student suffer, and laugh in their faces when they asked pity for their pain. *He* would have asked no pity, and his pain was greater than theirs. Go on, girl, he whispered, as the student, facing her implacable ill will, sighed and wept. Go on, girl. One day he would talk like that, he would face them and tell them how much he hated them, how they had made him suffer, how he would pay them back!

How, one must surely wonder, does this image relate to Baldwin's personal confrontation with the South, no less than with the specific and recurrent images of lynchings previously addressed? First, the intensity and instinctive knowingness of John's identification with a defiant and fallen woman begs a simple question. Why her? Her pride is the courageous pride of those individuals who, against all odds and obstacles, fight back and say, to recall Melville, in the midst of the "personified impersonal," a personality stands here. The woman's point of view represents the serious artist's point of view by which he or she will prosper or fail, live or perish. And in John's instance, like Baldwin's and those of numerous others, this point of view must be embraced with vitality and vigilance. Thus, John empathizes and appropriates the woman's vision. Disregarding her ugly and troubling circumstances, he cheers her on: "Go on, girl. One day he would talk like that, he would face them and tell them how much he hated them, how they made him suffer, how he would pay them back!"[27]

John Grimes, with such power, could free himself from the nightmare of history represented by his father's house, the nightmare of history that includes the southern threat and horror of emasculation and death. He could thereby become the master of his fate, a principal actor in the creation of his own reality.

Like John, Baldwin began early on to negate the power of his southern stepfather and later that of another powerful Southerner and surrogate father, Richard Wright. He would allow neither to compromise his attempt to create an original literary space for himself. It is useful to bear in mind some of Baldwin's own comments on escaping the nightmare of history. It may even prove an exercise in futility, he warns us. Why? We are fatally "trapped in history," no less than "history is trapped in us." Nevertheless, the writer must always make an attempt to free himself or herself through periodic gestures of eloquence. And Baldwin brilliantly succeeded. Writing became the agency, the holy spirit, by which Baldwin transformed history. And by this same agency and spirit, he was released from the tyranny of his father's house. He built a castle of his own and imagined a world and a point of view that took him far beyond the confines of his father's dogmatically religious view of the world and the limitations imposed by peculiarly American dilemmas involving race and sexuality. He translated his choice of vocation and his concomitant search for a new form of empowerment and fulfillment into Art. To borrow a phrase from his mentor Henry James, his life involved *par excellence* "the madness of art." And through the mad agency of Art, he perpetually attempted to create another culture, another country, another world. He tried, to use his own words, "to end the racial nightmare, achieve our country and change the history of the world."[28]

NOTES

1 Horace Porter, *Stealing the Fire: The Art and Protest of James Baldwin* (Middletown, CT: Wesleyan University Press, 1989).
2 Ibid., p. 16.
3 Fred L. Standley and Lewis H. Pratt, eds., *Conversations with James Baldwin* (Jackson: University of Mississippi Press, 1989), p. 202.
4 David Leeming, *James Baldwin* (New York: Alfred A. Knopf,1994), pp. 137–141.
5 James Baldwin, *The Price of the Ticket* (New York: St. Martin's, 1985), p. 184.
6 Ibid., p. 184.
7 Ibid., p. 485.
8 Ibid., p. 487.
9 Ibid., p. 487.
10 Ibid., p. 488.
11 Ibid., p. 142.
12 James Baldwin, *Go Tell It on the Mountain* (New York: The Dial Press, 1953), p. 9.
13 Ibid., p. 19.

14 Ibid., p. 19.
15 Ibid., p. 19.
16 Ibid., p. 20.
17 Ibid., p. 35.
18 For a thorough discussion of this, see Porter, *Stealing the Fire*, pp. 15–20.
19 James Baldwin, *Go Tell It on the Mountain*, p. 161.
20 Ibid., p. 161.
21 Ibid., p. 161.
22 James Baldwin, *Going to Meet the Man* (New York: Dell Publishing, 1966), p. 216.
23 Trudier Harris, *Exorcising Blackness: Historical and Literary Lynching and Burning Rituals* (Bloomington: University of Indiana Press, 1984), p. xi.
24 David Leeming, *James Baldwin*, p. 248.
25 Baldwin, *Go Tell It on the Mountain*, p. 39.
26 Ibid., p. 41.
27 Ibid., p. 42.
28 Baldwin, *The Price of the Ticket*, p. 379.

4

Wrestling with "The Love That Dare Not Speak Its Name": John, Elisha, and the "Master"

BRYAN R. WASHINGTON

I

EARLY in *Go Tell It on the Mountain,* when John's mother says, "The Lord'll reveal to you in His own good time everything He wants you to know," we are told that "he had heard her say this before – it was her text."[1] John, however, has yet to discover what *his* text is. He ultimately embraces scripture, but the novel as a whole has as much invested in Henry James's tradition as it does in the Bible. I have argued elsewhere that *Giovanni's Room* (1956) makes homosexual desire explicit in James by revising "The Beast in the Jungle" (1902).[2] In *Go Tell It on the Mountain,* the situation is reversed. James, in effect, silences Baldwin.

By the turn of the century, James had the reputation of being an exacting literary craftsman. His most avid supporters, among them Hendrik Andersen, Jocelyn Persse, and Hugh Walpole, proclaimed him the "Master." What began as private obeisance has become a widespread critical convention, one that perpetuates the problematic and generally unchallenged assumption that James is a writer who rightfully commands unquestioning loyalty from all who read him. Accorded the canonical status of a sovereign, he oversees a vast literary dominion. That Baldwin, who greatly admired him, wrestled with his authority at crucial points throughout his career, is the underlying premise of this essay. Indeed, the troubled nature of his discipleship, or his indenture, is particularly evident in his first novel. For what James refuses to say Baldwin will not say either. On the authority of the "Master," in other words, homosexuality must go unspoken. And yet its very namelessness is its name.

C. W. E. Bigsby argues that "the potential love between John and Elisha, lightly sketched and providing only the barest of possibilities, bears no relationship to the white world which dispossesses both of them."[3] Bigsby appears to suggest that the specter of homosexuality in Baldwin's first novel points up his lack of interest in social protest. On these terms, literary homosexuality is a narrative self-indulgence, a textual retreat from the reality of white racism. But, whatever their sexual orientation, Baldwin's blacks are always conscious of white culture – which, as he maintains in work after work, is inescapable. And his gay characters, black and white, are doubly oppressed: They must contend not only with racism, but also with homophobia. Although Bigsby is not a gay studies theorist, his impatience with *Go Tell It on the Mountain*'s sexual ambiguity anticipates contemporary gay critical approaches to this text in particular and to Baldwin in general – approaches in which irritation and frustration predominate. In elaborating on why homosexuality in Baldwin's first novel is so deeply buried (or so methodically disguised), I shall also consider the role recent gay theorists, specifically white gay theorists, expect Baldwin to play. For it seems that because he is black, his texts must be free of the repressive impulses characterizing either the work of his gay contemporaries or that of his gay precursors.

Baldwin figures prominently in three important contributions to gay theory. Claude J. Summers's *Gay Fictions, Wilde to Stonewall* includes an essay on *Giovanni's Room*, arguing that it "is a central text . . . in the American literature of homosexuality."[4] *Go Tell It on the Mountain*'s canonical status, on the other hand, is questionable because race, rather than sexuality, is allegedly its primary preoccupation. What Summers fails to see is that blackness and homosexuality in Baldwin are not simply coterminous; they are virtually interchangeable. For example, David's oppression as a homosexual in *Giovanni's Room* immediately aligns itself with the persecution of African-Americans: "My ancestors conquered a continent, pushing across death-laden plains, until they came to an ocean which faced away from Europe into a darker past."[5] In *Gaiety Transfigured*, David Bergman grapples with Baldwin's refusal to accept the classification of "gay writer."[6] Once again, blackness and homosexuality are polarized, an approach that partially explains Bergman's troubling revalorization of the infamous *Notes of a Native Son,* in which Eldridge Cleaver reproves Baldwin both for his sexual orientation and for the homosexual themes undergirding his work. For the purposes of this essay, however, Lee Edelman is perhaps the most important gay theorist writing today. The brilliant, though frequently disturbing, *Homographesis* argues in a chapter on Baldwin that he typically portrays black men as the helpless victims of repressed white homosexuals. To Edelman, these representations only serve to reinforce homosexual and (by implication) racial stereotypes.[7] In other words, when black writers construct scenes in which white men force or attempt to force themselves on black men, they imply that interracial homosexual acts always involve a loss of power (and indeed of subjectivity) for the black male. But to chide Baldwin, and other black writers as well (among them, Toni Morrison),[8] for the moments in their work when homosexuality is associated with white racism is to suggest that whites have been misrepresented, that they are not the oppressors. If whiteness in American culture is not the emblem of power and aggression, what is it? Why, in short, would black writers conceive whites differently?

That blackness is peculiarly vulnerable to, has indeed been invaded by, forces outside it is a central idea in Baldwin's work. This is the thesis, for example, of "Stranger in the Village" (1953), the signal essay published the same year *Go Tell It on the Mountain* appeared. Even though many of the inhabitants of the unnamed Swiss village Baldwin describes are unable to read, they nevertheless "have made the modern world."

> The most illiterate among them is related, in a way that I am not, to Dante, Shakespeare, Michelangelo, Aeschylus, Da Vinci, Rembrandt, and Racine; the cathedral at Chartres says something to them which it cannot say to me. . . . Out of their hymns and dances come Beethoven and Bach. Go back a few centuries and they are in their full glory – but I am in Africa, watching the conquerors arrive. ("Stranger in the Village" 83)

Imposing itself on African-Americans, white culture both "controls" Baldwin and "has even in a sense, created" ("Stranger in the Village" 82) him. White conquest is not only crucial to this essay, but, as we have seen, it is also important for *Giovanni's Room,* in which David identifies himself from the start as the descendant of colonizers. Even Eric – the white bisexual in *Another Country* (1962) who as a child understood white people as "cold" and black people as "warm . . . and as necessary as the sun"[9] – is a sexual invader. He is attracted to Rufus, the black jazz musician who ultimately kills himself, because Rufus reminds him of black workers he had watched as a child: "dark men, seen briefly, somewhere, in a garden or clearing, . . . , sweat running down their chocolate chests and shoulders, . . . , the white of their jock-straps beautiful against their skin."[10] Lamenting the fact that Baldwin's gayness does not result in a forgiving figuration of white sexual minorities, Edelman accuses him of homophobia, but in the final analysis the real charge brought against him is racism. Baldwin equates whiteness with power; Edelman, insisting on his own disenfranchisement, does not. The critical need to universalize the experience of all minorities thus becomes intensely disturbing.

Part One of *Go Tell It on the Mountain* investigates not only black disempowerment, but also black self-hatred. John associates cognitive power, for example, with whiteness. At school, the validation of his abilities he values most comes from whites:

> It was not only colored people who praised John, since they could not, John felt, in any case really know; but white people also said it, in fact had said it first and said it still. It was when John was five years old and in the first grade that he was first noticed; and since he was noticed by an eye altogether alien and impersonal, began to perceive, in wild uneasiness, his individual existence. (20)

The "alien" eye in question is that of the school principal, "a [white] woman, with white hair and an iron face, [who] look[s] down at him" (20). Self-perception, in John's case, is thus conferred; it is the impartation of the white other, the result of her gaze. Books, too, are associated with whiteness, with power. The

New York Public Library is to John a white cultural citadel that he one day hopes to invade:

> [It is] a building filled with books and unimaginably vast, and which he had never yet dared to enter. He might, he knew, for he was a member of the branch in Harlem and was entitled to take books from any library in the city. But he had never gone in because the building was so big that it must be full of corridors and marble steps, in the maze of which he would be lost and never find the book he wanted. And then everyone, all the white people inside, would know that he was not used to great buildings, or to many books, and they would look at him with pity. He would enter on another day, when he had read all the books uptown, an achievement that would, he felt, lend him the poise to enter any building in the world. (37)

Because his work so frequently responds to white canonical texts, Baldwin is the kind of reader that John aspires to become. Arguably, the Baldwinian dialogue with whiteness is at its most powerful when James enters the discursive terrain. In *The Politics of Exile,* I suggest that Baldwin either capitulates to the authority of the "Master" or undermines it by revising and/or recontextualizing his narrative preoccupations. *Go Tell It on the Mountain,* as we shall see, is a novel in which submission to James's dictates is the dominant mode because it evades or covers over homosexuality.

Dividing black writers into two camps, Edelman points to those who argue that homosexuality "is a form of white decadence" (Edelman 59) and to those who maintain that homophobia is the legacy of whites:

> Both pronouncements . . . identify something external in its essence, whether homosexuality or homophobia, as imposing itself on an alarmingly receptive African-American community so that in each case the issue to be engaged is the perceived vulnerability of the (communal) black body to (ideological) penetration by whites. (Edelman 59)

I would suggest that, especially in *Go Tell It on the Mountain,* it is difficult to assign Baldwin to either category. For he is unable to decide how to rescue homosexuality, for which James's texts provide the model, from homophobia, for which James also provides the model. What is particularly disturbing about Edelman's argument is the suggestion that the way Baldwin represents white aggression is a function of his paranoia:

> The metaphorics of colonization give voice to a paranoia – however justifiable – characteristically marked by the anxious-making confusion of inside and outside, self and other. Whether those black nationalists and Afrocentrists who denounce homosexuality among African-Americans read it as a passive internalization of the oppressor's alien practices, and thus as a potentially genocidal subversion of a "natural" black masculinity, their gay-affirmative counterparts interpret such homophobic attitudes as themselves betraying the internalization of a "foreign" practice that undermines the specificity of black cultural experience. (Edelman 59)

All this assumes that Baldwin conceives blackness and whiteness as irrevocably divided when, instead, on his terms they are irrevocably intertwined. Of Baldwin's final novel *Just Above My Head* (1979), Edelman argues that the "novel appropriates from Du Bois his awareness of the painful division and alienation of a self-consciousness always already 'doubled' as the mark of its penetration – indeed, its constitution – by the other: a doubling or division assuring that the judgments we 'are' come always from somewhere else" (Edelman 62). In this reading of Du Bois, posited as Baldwin's as well, the other, however despised, plays an organizing role in the construction of a unified black identity. In other words, blackness cannot exist without whiteness, but white culture is invested in perpetuating the arbitrary boundary between black and white. Baldwin is not so motivated. He insists that the boundary collapsed the moment blacks were ripped away from Africa and transported to the West. Thus he argues in "Stranger in the Village" that the community he inhabits is finally "the West, the West onto which . . . [he has] been so strangely grafted."[11] Although Du Bois's importance for Baldwin is undeniable, he revises *The Souls of Black Folk* (1903) so that blackness and whiteness converge rather than divide in African-Americans. For as Baldwin argues in "Here Be Dragons" (originally published as "Freaks and the American Ideal of Manhood" in 1985), the "object of one's hatred is never, alas, conveniently outside but is seated in one's lap, stirring in one's bowels and dictating the beat of one's heart."[12]

Since Edelman reads this complicated passage as quintessentially homophobic because it appears to suggest that homosexuality is an act of white aggression, it is important to read it with its context in mind. Baldwin refers to his early experience with the New York "gay world" (PT 686), a world he describes as alienating because of the racial and sexual stereotypes operating within it. "[T]he very last thing this black boy needed," he writes, "were clouds of imitation white women and speculations concerning the size of his organ" (PT 686). Arguing that he was exploited "by people who truly meant . . . [him] no harm" (PT 686), he quickly points out that "they could *not* have meant him any harm because they did not see . . . [him]" (PT 686). Baldwin's problem is thus not a question of divided identity, but one of a controlling desire for recognition from the other. Significantly, he writes that it is "very dangerous to model one's opposition to the arbitrary definition, the imposed ordeal, merely on the example supplied by one's oppressor" (PT 686). It is at this point that he identifies the oppressor's location, figuring him as both lover and rapist. That the oppressor is sometimes the object of desire, "dictating the beat of one's heart," is precisely the paradox with which Baldwin wrestled throughout his career. It will become clear that *Go Tell It on the Mountain* assigns several meanings to the figure of the wrestling match.

In Edelman's view, *Just Above My Head* is what *Go Tell It on the Mountain* should have been. Even though their relationship ultimately fails, Arthur and Crunch are sexually liberated; John and Elisha are not:

> Baldwin does more than merely acknowledge the eros inhabiting the language of religious surrender and redemption – an acknowledgment upon which he predicated the ambiguous resolution of *Go Tell It On the Mountain*. He suggests, beyond this, that the "new" identity into which Arthur and Crunch can be born again is one mutually determining and relational, effected not through a fortification of boundaries but through a willingness to allow the boundaries of their identities to be penetrated. (Edelman 69)

But, as I am about to suggest, it is the absence of an unambiguous prior textual model for structuring a homosexual relationship that prevents John and Elisha from becoming Arthur and Crunch. Given its historical context, *Go Tell It on the Mountain*'s repressed homosexuality is perhaps easily explained. It is the product of a period in which homosexuality was not a subject for public debate. On the other hand, *Giovanni's Room,* appearing only three years later, is a clear, if problematic, articulation of homosexual desire, though it is highly critical of the gay community. The implication in "Here Be Dragons" that the gay community Baldwin knew as a young man was dominated by effeminate white men conditioned to define black men wholly in terms of the proportions of their genitalia may strike some as a dangerous generalization and as yet another example of his homophobia. In this essay the specific concern is gay life in the 1940s – precisely the period, in short, when Baldwin began to write.

Arguably, *Go Tell It on the Mountain* is a comment on the difficulty of coming to terms with homosexuality in a repressive environment. But, at the risk of dehistoricizing Baldwin's work, I suggest that the explanation for the figuration of homosexuality in this early text, one that so many critics find disturbing today, lies in material coming much later. Consider, for example, his 1984 interview with Richard Goldstein. Asked whether he sees himself as a "stranger in gay America," Baldwin replies that

> The word gay has always rubbed me the wrong way. I never understood exactly what is meant by it. . . . I simply feel that it's a world that has very little to do with me, with where I did my growing up. I was never at home in it. Even in my early years in the Village, what I saw of that world absolutely frightened me, bewildered me. I didn't understand the necessity of all the role playing. And in a way I still don't.[13]

Baldwin's point is that the so-called gay community has yet to establish an identity that does not rely on parodies of heterosexual conventions. Not surprisingly, he also indicts the "community" for its racism, arguing that "the gay world as such is no more prepared to accept black people than anywhere else in society. It's a very hermetically sealed world with very unattractive features, including racism" (Goldstein 14). But what I find particularly compelling about this interview are Goldstein's own revelations. "I sometimes think," he says, "[that] gay people look to black people as healing them . . . [,] healing their alienation . . . , conferring a kind of acceptance by embracing them in a coalition" (Goldstein 14). As a black critic presented with the challenge of responding to recent readings of Baldwin, I have been unable to avoid the unhappy conclusion that white gay theory is disturbingly self-interested, that it looks to Baldwin for absolution and disciplines him when he refuses to give it. In this regard, Goldstein's candor is quite helpful, for he openly states what is only implied in the criticism I have mentioned: "I feel distinct from other white people" (Goldstein 14).

II

Although *Go Tell It on the Mountain* is not a novel conceived as a salve for white liberal guilt, white culture – as with "Here Be Dragons" – is figured both as an "object . . . of hatred" and as an object of desire. I have said that John has yet to discover what his text is. In a novel that will not (cannot) articulate homosexual desire, there is a mechanism at work that implicates homosexuality by embracing (or possibly submitting to) a writer, celebrated as the "Master" of his craft, whose work is "stirring in the bowels" of Baldwin's text. Though John and Elisha's climactic alliance is anti-climactic in the (homo)sexual sense, it nevertheless points toward a textual relationship, which Baldwin simultaneously invites and fends off, that returns us to his idea of the intimacy black and white texts share. Welcome or unwelcome, James penetrates *Go Tell It On the Mountain,* urging silence and yet at the same time releasing his (homo)sexual codes.

Here I am indebted to Eve Kosofsky Sedgwick's *Epistemology of the Closet.* Tracing patterns in James's work that compare with those of other writers of his period, Sedgwick reminds us that, historically, Christianity had always named homosexuality by not naming it. In the annals of Protestants and Catholics alike, she writes, it is "Unspeakable, Unmentionable, *nefandam libidi-*

nem, 'that sin which should be neither named nor committed,' the 'detestable and abominable sin, amongst Christians not to be named.' "[14] This is precisely what happens in *Go Tell It on the Mountain:* John's sin, his love for Elisha, cannot be named; it can only be transcribed into a spiritual battle between self-love and unquestioning devotion to God's will. Sedgwick points out that the Christian practice of not naming "the sin" had become, by the time Oscar Wilde was convicted on sodomy charges in 1895, a secular convention as well. It was Lord Alfred Douglas, Wilde's erratic and ultimately selfish lover, who penned the famous line, "I am the love that dare not speak its name."[15] At roughly the turn of the century, then, the unspeakable had already come to be "more firmly and distinctively [packed] with homosexual meaning" (Sedgwick 203). "The Beast in the Jungle" appeared seven years after Wilde's conviction. If in this tale James responds to public outrage at the revelations unleashed during the Wilde trials by implicitly advocating a return to the way things were, it should not surprise us that Baldwin does much the same thing in a novel focusing on black Pentecostal culture, a culture as repressive (albeit differently so) as James's English bourgeoisie.

John Marcher is in an emotional, but finally unspecified, state of panic. Middle-aged and unmarried, he leads a barren existence. His friendship with May Bartram, whom he has known for years, is his primary intimacy (in the social sense), but it is utterly passionless. Sedgwick makes a convincing case for the homosexual meaning of, for example, Marcher's "secret,"[16] "his queer consciousness" (Sedgwick 511), "his unhappy perversion" (Sedgwick 499). John Grimes is not a middle-aged man, and yet his anxieties are similarly figured. Playing in Central Park, he nearly "knock[s] down an old white man with a white beard" (34). Rather than reprimand him, the man smiles: "John smiled back. It was as though he and the old man had between them a great *secret* [emphasis added]" (34–35). We are also told that his "secret heart had flourished in its wickedness until the day his sin overtook him" (21). He is particularly drawn to "a green metal serpent" – Satan? a phallus? both? – displayed on the family mantelpiece (27). And:

He had sinned. In spite of the saints, his mother and his father, the warnings he had heard from his earliest beginnings, he had sinned with his hands a sin that was hard to forgive. In the school lavatory, alone, thinking of the boys, older, bigger, braver, who made bets with each other as to whose urine could arch higher, he had watched in himself a transformation of which he would never dare to speak. (18–19)

It is tempting to read all this as evidence for the tension between John's heterosexual awakening and his desire to be "saved," which necessitates forfeiting mere physical pleasure for spiritual ecstasy. The "transformation of which he would never dare to speak" becomes a terrified and indoctrinated adolescent's response to the taboo of sexual self-gratification. Immediately before this, Baldwin writes that "John wondered at his panic . . . (while the yellow stain on the ceiling slowly transformed itself into a woman's nakedness" (18). But when John invokes a woman, his thoughts turn quickly to men – to, that is, the "older, bigger, braver" boys whose athletic and (by implication) sexual prowess are his obsession. Male-male desire is thus not only mediated, legitimated, by the figure of a woman, but it is also defined in terms of conventional heterosexual equations: power is male; powerlessness is female. In other words, John's unspoken desire for men suggests, to reinvoke Baldwin's interview with Goldstein, that he is (or is resigned to function as) an "imitation" woman.

A similar triangular configuration comes into play when, in Part One, John visits a Sixth Avenue cinema. A large movie poster depicting "a wicked woman, half undressed . . . [and] apparently quarreling with a blond man" (37) mesmerizes him. We are told that "he felt identified with the blond young man, the fool of his family" (37), but once the film begins, the figure with whom he feels "identified" shifts from male to female. Although Baldwin does not name it, the film John finds so enthralling is *Of Human Bondage* (1934), which made Bette Davis a star. Based on Somerset Maugham's best-selling novel, this is the somewhat melodramatic tale of a young medical student obsessed with a woman incapable of fidelity. Full of her signature gestures, Davis's highly stylized performance comes close to camp. There can be little doubt that Baldwin was aware of Davis's almost mythic status within the gay community. Even today, drag queens and female impersonators routinely imitate her. Lines from her films are still central to the gay vernacular, and the echo of her unmistakable diction remains ubiquitous. As *Go Tell It on the Mountain* suggests, the reasons behind gay fascination with Davis are complex. Part of her appeal involves the threat she represents, in role after role, to heterosexual male authority. On the whole, her work is combative, impatient with Hollywood gender stereotypes.

Viewing *Of Human Bondage*, John witnesses a woman whose defiance of convention is so aggressive, and thus so dangerous, that the film ultimately sentences her to death:

> She had a great many boy friends, and she smoked cigarettes and drank. When she met the young man, who was a student and who loved her very much, she was very cruel to him. She laughed at him because he was a cripple. She took his money and she went out with other men, and she lied to the student – who was certainly a fool. He limped about, looking soft and sad, and soon all John's sympathy was given to this violent and unhappy woman. He understood her when she raged and shook her hips and threw back her head in laughter so furious that it seemed the veins of her neck would burst. She walked the cold foggy streets, a little woman and not pretty, with a lewd, brutal swagger, saying to the whole world: "You can kiss my ass." (39)

The complication here is that in his search for an alternative masculinity, John ends up valorizing a woman who acts like a man. Rejecting the example of the "soft and sad" male, he resolves "to be like her,"

> only more powerful, more thorough, and more cruel; to make those around him, all who hurt him, suffer as she made the student suffer, and laugh in their faces when they asked pity for pain. . . . Go on, girl, he whispered, as the student, facing her implacable ill will, sighed and wept. Go on girl. One day he would talk like that, he would face them and tell them how much he hated them, how they had made him suffer, how he would pay them back. (39)

But what does the desire to "talk like that" mean? Are we to conclude that John's voice, his identity, will be homosexual? Or does Baldwin lament the absence of models for young men who depart from the masculinist norm? For, clearly, what John finds compelling about the Davis character is her power. The male figure, in this instance, is powerless and in tears.

John is particularly adept at performing traditionally female tasks. It is he, for example, who cleans the house, sweeping, polishing, "excavat[ing], as it were, from the dust that threatened to bury them, his family's goods and gear" (27). But John's skill within the domestic sphere becomes a comment on the novel's frustration with the values assigned to "male" and "female." For John despises the work he so skillfully performs:

> [He] hated sweeping this carpet, for dust rose, clogging his nose and sticking to his sweaty skin, and he felt that he could sweep it forever, the clouds of dust would not diminish, the rug would not be clean. It became in his imagination his impossible, lifelong task, his hard trial, like that of a man he read about somewhere, whose curse it was to push a boulder up a steep hill, only to have the giant who guarded the hill roll the boulder down again – and so on, forever, throughout eternity. (26)

Imagining John as a domestic Sisyphus, Baldwin makes it clear that he has been punished for the "sin" of being different. Looking into the mirror he has been cleaning, John does not confront "the hand of Satan," which is "as yet invisible" (27). But there is the suggestion that it may soon appear, for the allusion to *The Picture of Dorian Gray* (1891) is unmistakable. Like Wilde's protagonist, John has a face that will not betray his "sins." And yet this is also "the face of a stranger, a stranger who held secrets that John could never know" (27). It is a face for which he has no reference, a configuration of "details . . . [whose] principle of . . . unity . . . [is] undiscoverable" (27). But insofar as it suggests a homosexual identity, this is a face that Baldwin obviously recognizes; hence, the text accords John the very kind of interpretive protection that James extends to Marcher. One can easily read this moment before the mirror as an attestation to John's conviction that he will never live up to the example of Elisha, who has already been saved. And similarly, it is just as easy to maintain, as so many have done, that James's tale is a heterosexual tragedy in which what is finally recognized is that recognition has come too late.

Among the boys who delight in stickball, John is an alien who cannot "play their games" (30). And yet he yearns "to be with these boys in the street, heedless and thoughtless, wearing out his treacherous and bewildering body" (30). Assuming that James's codes are embedded in Baldwin's text, John's desire to wear out his body is not unlike Marcher's desperate yearning for emotional and arguably for physical penetration at the end of "The Beast in the Jungle." I refer to the famous graveyard scene in which Marcher observes a man so overwhelmed with grief that he realizes his own life has been meaningless: "No passion had ever touched him, for this was what passion meant; he had survived and maundered and pined, but where had been *his* deep ravage?" (James 534).

Marcher's unchecked voyeurism, his intense fascination with the nameless mourner, becomes important for this reading of *Go Tell It on the Mountain*. For John Grimes is a watcher of men too, constantly measuring himself against them. Just as James's mourner is the man Marcher wishes he could be, so Elisha is the role model whose "arrival had caused . . . John's mood to change" (51). Hence, the importance of their initial wrestling match:

> Usually such a battle was soon over, since Elisha was so much bigger and stronger and as a wrestler so much more skilled; but tonight John was filled with a determination not to be conquered, or at least to make the conquest dear. With all the strength that was in him he fought against Elisha, and he was filled with a strength that was almost hatred. . . . [T]he odor of Elisha's sweat was heavy in John's nostrils. He saw the veins rise on Elisha's forehead and in his neck; his breath became jagged and harsh, and the grimace on his face became more cruel; and John, watching these manifestations of his power, was filled with a wild delight. (52–53)

On the simplest level, this is John's first opportunity to prove his manhood by overpowering the older Elisha, by beating him at his own game. But what begins as sport quickly suggests a sexual encounter. Though they do not have a name for it, John and

Elisha are wrestling with homosexual desire. And so, as a novelist, is Baldwin who, in coming so close to making it explicit, runs the risk of writing himself out of the "Master's" tradition. In Part Three homosexual desire is present only in the sense that John's conversion refers to the first wrestling match. But John is now Jacob, Elisha his angel, and the phallus the rod of God. Saved, John has been "invaded, set at naught, possessed" (193). That is his "deep ravage." And in response, Elisha presses his lips to his forehead, giving him "a *holy* kiss" (221, emphasis added).

I have indicated that there are moments in the text when the suggestion of homosexual desire depends on the intervention of a female figure. And thus John's admiration for Elisha begins to surface when he notices the way Elisha reacts to Ella Mae. Indeed, Elisha and Ella Mae are disciplined before the entire congregation for their "disorderly" (16) display of affection. And the minister who gives them their "public warning" (17) is none other than Father James, arguably Henry James transcribed into a black man.

If Baldwin blackens the "Master," then he acknowledges James's role in shaping his own narrative project. Most critics who consider Baldwin's indebtedness to James focus on the numerous occasions when his work pays homage to his forms.[17] So, for example, in deference to *The Golden Bowl* (1904), the story of a disintegrating marriage divided into two sections ("The Prince" and "The Princess"), *Giovanni's Room* splits in half, thus appropriating James's frustration with the discord and alienation that, he suggests, are inherent in heterosexual (and by implication) in homosexual relationships as well. Similarly, *Go Tell It on the Mountain* divides into three parts, its structure mirroring the competing desires (familial, racial, and sexual) operating throughout it.

Although on one level the figure of Father James works as a marker for Baldwin's commitment to Henry James's overall aesthetic, on another it throws into relief his attempt both to situate himself within the "Master's" tradition and to open it up in order to insert blackness. In the well-known "Criticism in the Jungle," Henry Louis Gates, Jr., argues that in the case of the writer of African descent, her or his texts occupy spaces in at least two traditions: a European or American literary tradition, and one of the several related but distinct black traditions. The "heritage" of each black text written in a Western language is, then, a double heritage, two-toned, as it were. Its visual tones are white and black, and its aural tones are standard and vernacular.[18]

Barbara Johnson suggests that this pronouncement revalorizes Du Bois's argument that "the black man's [emphasis removed] soul is divided in two."[19] But, as I have already implied, *Go Tell It on the Mountain* challenges the notion that black identity is fractured. In this regard, Father James is paradigmatic, for he is both black and white. The significance of the passage to which I am about to turn thus depends on the conflation of two discourses: black Protestant oratory and Henry James's genteel narrative prescriptions, both of which, as far as (homo)sexuality is concerned, are repressive:

> It was not an easy thing, said Father James, to be the pastor of a flock. It might look easy to just sit up there in the pulpit night after night, year in, year out, but let them remember the awful responsibility placed on his shoulders by almighty God – let them remember that God would ask an accounting of him one day for every soul in his flock. Let them remember that the Word was hard, that the way of holiness was a hard way. There was no room in God's army for the coward heart, no crown awaiting him who put mother, or father, sister, or brother, sweetheart, or friend above God's will. Let the church cry amen to this! (17)

My point is that the novel labors to serve two masters, each of whom demands complete obedience to the "hard" "Word," be it the word of God or the word(s) of a writer who, by the time Baldwin began to write, had a godlike reputation (in some intellectual quarters) when it came to the art of the novel. Baldwin's dual allegiance will not permit the full disclosure, the complete articulation, of a looming homosexual alliance. For Father James's excoriation implicates not only Elisha and Ella Mae, but also John. As we have seen, "no crown await[s] him who put mother, or father, sister, or brother, sweetheart, or *friend* [emphasis added] above God's will." In short, the intentionally repressed homosexual meaning undergirding the whole of the Father James sequence depends on its point of view – on, that is, John's voyeurism:

> Elisha, who was tall and handsome, who played basketball, and who had been saved at the age of eleven in the improbable fields down south. *Had* he sinned? Had he been tempted? And the girl beside him, whose white robes now seemed the merest, thinnest covering for the nakedness of breasts and insistent thighs – what was her face like when she was one with Elisha, with no singing, when they were not surrounded by the saints? He was afraid to think of it, yet he could think of nothing else; and the fever of which they stood accused began also to rage in him. (17)

As René Girard maintains, "true jealousy . . . always contains an element of fascination with the insolent rival."[20] Ella Mae naked is not simply an object of desire in John's eyes, but a sexual threat precisely because she possesses what he does not: a woman's body. Which is not to say that he wishes for breasts or for "insistent" thighs, but rather that he supposes that *Elisha* is drawn to, and possibly has witnessed, female nakedness. Forbidden to see each other "each day after school," Elisha and Ella Mae have the option, nevertheless, of entering a union authorized by the church: "If they came together again it would be in wedlock. They would have children and raise them in the church" (17).

For John, however, the way to Elisha's bed is unauthor(iz)ed. Re-enforcing the convention of not naming homosexuality, Baldwin is unable to construct a scenario in which the desire to be *like* another man could become the uncoded desire to be *with* another man:

> What were the thoughts of Elisha when night came, and he was alone where no eye could see, and no tongue bear witness, save only the trumpetlike tongue of God? Were his thoughts, his bed, his body foul? What were his dreams? (60)

The textual tradition(s) out of which *Go Tell It on the Mountain* emerges does not tell us.

NOTES

1 James Baldwin, *Go Tell It on the Mountain* (New York: Laurel, 1985), p. 32. Subsequent page references are to this edition.

2 See Washington, "The Beast in *Giovanni's Room*," in *The Politics of Exile: Ideology in Henry James, F. Scott Fitzgerald, and James Baldwin* (Boston: Northeastern University Press, 1995), pp. 70–91.

3 C. W. E Bigsby, "The Divided Mind of James Baldwin," in Hollis R. Lynch, ed., *The Second Black Renaissance: Essays in Black Literature*, Contributions in Afro-American and African Studies 50 (Westport, CT: Greenwood Press, 1980), p. 122.

4 See Claude J. Summers, " 'Looking at the Naked Sun': James Baldwin's *Giovanni's Room*," in *Gay Fictions, Wilde to Stonewall: Studies in a Male Homosexual Literary Tradition* (New York: Continuum, 1990), p. 172.

5 James Baldwin, *Giovanni's Room* (New York: Dial, 1956).

6 See David Bergman, "The Agony of Gay Black Literature," in *Gaiety Transfigured: Gay Self-Representation in American Literature* (Madison: University of Wisconsin Press, 1991), pp. 163–187.

7 Lee Edelman, "The Part for the (W)hole: Baldwin, Homophobia, and the Fantasmatics of 'Race'," in *Homographesis: Essays in Gay Literary and Cultural Theory* (New York: Routledge, 1994), pp. 42–75. Subsequent page references are to this edition.

8 Edelman specifically refers to Morrison's *Beloved* and to Frantz Fanon's *Black Skin, White Masks*.

9 James Baldwin, *Another Country* (New York: Dial, 1962), pp. 193–194.

10 Ibid., p. 194.

11 James Baldwin, "Stranger in the Village," in *The Price of the Ticket: Collected Nonfiction, 1948–1985* (hereafter PT) (New York: St. Martin's, 1985), p. 83. Subsequent page references are to this edition.

12 James Baldwin, "Here Be Dragons," in *The Price of the Ticket*, p. 686.

13 Richard Goldstein, " 'Go the Way Your Blood Beats': An Interview with James Baldwin," *Village Voice* 26 (June 1984): 13. Subsequent page references are to this issue.

14 Quoted in Eve Kosofsky Sedgwick, *Epistemology of the Closet* (Berkeley and Los Angeles: University of California Press, 1990), p. 202 (from John Boswell's *Christianity, Social Tolerance, and Homosexuality* and from Alan Bray's *Homosexuality in Renaissance England*).

15 Quoted in Sedgwick, p. 74 (from the poem "Two Loves," 1894). See also Richard Ellmann's account of Wilde's first trial in *Oscar*

Wilde (New York: Knopf, 1987), p. 463. Douglas's poem was integral to the prosecution's case.

16 Henry James, "The Beast in the Jungle," in *Selected Fiction*, Leon Edel, ed. (New York: Dutton, 1964), p. 507. Subsequent page references are to this edition.

17 See Charles Newman, "The Lesson of the Master: Henry James and James Baldwin," *Yale Review* 56 (October 1966): 45–46; and Horace Porter, *Stealing the Fire: The Art and Protest of James Baldwin* (Middletown, CT: Wesleyan University Press, 1989), pp. 125–153.

18 Henry Louis Gates, Jr., "Criticism in the Jungle," in *Black Literature and Literary Theory*, Henry Louis Gates, Jr., ed. (New York: Methuen, 1984), p. 4.

19 Barbara Johnson, "Metaphor, Metonymy, and Voice in *Their Eyes Were Watching God*," in *A World of Difference* (Baltimore: Johns Hopkins University Press, 1987), p. 167.

20 René Girard, *Deceit, Desire, and the Novel*, trans. Yvonne Freccero (Baltimore: Johns Hopkins University Press, 1965), p. 12.

5

Ambivalent Narratives, Fragmented Selves: Performative Identities and the Mutability of Roles in James Baldwin's *Go Tell It On the Mountain*

VIVIAN M. MAY

JAMES Baldwin's novel *Go Tell It on the Mountain* takes place in New York in the span of a weekend, mostly within the confines of a church and the Grimes family's house. The content of the novel, however, is not confined to actions in real time, for as the characters clean house or pray in church, they revisit and reconstruct the past and present through memories and feelings. Baldwin's oscillation between time frames, and between different characters' points of view, is very important: It provides readers with conflicting and fluctuating understandings of textual meaning. As readers we come away from the novel with a sense of ambivalence and irresolution, for the novel's discord is never harmonized. Baldwin explores ideas about the fragmented self and the mutability of human identity through this uncertainty. He invokes ambivalence by direct and indirect means. Sometimes parts of the novel directly contradict other parts, but occasionally discongruity occurs within and between those contradictions; Baldwin conveys uncertainty both by what he writes and what his characters say and by what he does not write and by what his characters do not say. Thus, for example, by alternating between the said and the unsaid, Baldwin interrogates both Gabriel's unmistakable drive to power and John's nebulous homosexual desire. Baldwin's text is constituted as much by what is not written as by what is written because the unwritten and invisible signify concepts, feelings, memories, and

desires that characters exclude from their conscious thoughts. Baldwin often links exclusion to characters' oppositional ways of looking at themselves and others: They believe that people are *either* good or evil, righteous or damned, but not both simultaneously. Through his characters, Baldwin invokes conventional oppositions in order to reveal their limited usefulness in exploring human identity.

Thus Baldwin critiques conventional notions of human identity invested in exclusionary thought processes and in oppositional dichotomies. He enacts a kaleidoscopic critique by employing narrative dissonance and cognitive ambivalence. Narrative dissonance means that both the reader and the novel's characters are confronted with different, conflicting narrations or reconstructions of events: What is "true" is unclear, as is who is "right." Baldwin's use of narrative discrepancies suggests a critique of conventional philosophical and religious notions of truth at the same time as it underscores how human identities are multifaceted and many-layered. For example, the convictions of Gabriel (the protagonist's father) and Esther (Gabriel's coworker down south) as to how their extramarital affair came about are very different: "Later, she told him that he had pursued her, that his eyes had left her not a moment's peace. 'That weren't no reverend looking at me them mornings in the yard,' she had said. 'You looked at me just like a man, like a man what hadn't never heard of the Holy Ghost.' But he believed that the Lord had laid her like a burden on his heart. . . . But she had not been thinking about God" (123). She believes that he chased and seduced her by using his power over her as a minister and as an older man, whereas he believes that she hounded and hunted him down while he was trying to convert her. Each character's summation of the dynamics behind his or her actions indicates discord: " 'Satan tempted me and I fell. I ain't the first man been made to fall on account of a wicked woman.' 'You be careful,' said Esther, 'how you talk to me. I ain't the first girl's been ruined by a holy man, neither' " (132). Whose interpretation is more true remains unresolved.

Less direct forms of narrative dissonance are also evident througout the novel. On the first page, the narrator describes

John's (the son) memories of the family's preparations for church, which

> were of the hurry and brightness of Sunday mornings. They all rose together on that day; his father, who did not have to go to work, and led them in prayer before breakfast; his mother, who dressed up on that day, and looked almost young . . . ; his younger brother, Roy, who was silent that day because his father was home. Sarah, who wore a red ribbon in her hair that day, and was fondled by her father. And the baby Ruth, who was dressed in pink and white, and rode in her mother's arms to church. (11)

The repetition of the phrase "that day" invokes both simple memory and a romantic reconstruction of the past. John's vision is rosy and warm. A page and a half later, however, readers confront quite a different interpretation. The second description contains contradictions both within itself and with the first one:

> The Grimes family arrived in a body, always a little late, usually in the middle of Sunday school. . . . This lateness was always their mother's fault – at least in the eyes of their father; she could not seem to get herself and the children ready on time, ever, and sometimes she actually remained behind, not to appear until the morning service. (13)

This passage evokes family tensions and blame, unlike the harmony of the first. Moreover, it is impossible for the family to "arrive in a body" if Elizabeth (John's mother) remains behind. The novel also closes with a disjuncture between coexisting interpretations of "reality." Sister Price and Sister McCandless believe that Elizabeth is crying because she is thinking about John having been saved: "Sister Price turned to look at her, and smiled. 'I know,' she said, 'you's a mighty happy woman this morning. . . . Yes, Lord . . . the Lord done raised you up a holy son. He going to comfort your gray hairs' " (208–209). Yet Elizabeth is thinking about her memories of Richard, and she starts to cry when she compares her meeting with Gabriel (her present husband) and her meeting with Richard (her first love): " *'Shake hands with the preacher, Johnny.' 'Got a man in the Bible, son, who liked music, too. . . . You reckon you going to dance before the Lord one of these days?' "* and *" 'You remember that day when you come into the store?' 'I didn't think you never looked at me.' 'Well – you was mighty pretty.' . . . 'What book was it, Richard?' 'Oh, I don't remember. Just a book.' 'You smiled.' 'You was mighty pretty' "* (209, 210). Discordant ruptures or gaps in the narrative, whether direct or indirect, signify the importance Baldwin places on multiple points of view; Baldwin elides a unified narrative through discursive dissemblance.

Cognitive ambivalence relates to narrative dissonance in that the characters are aware of these conflicting stories which are not resolved and do not "fit" neatly together under the rubric of one larger story or form of discourse. Yet for many of the characters, the desire for a unity of experience and a related unity of self is very strong: They want their experiences to fit neatly into certain paradigms (such as Christianity), thus they interpret past events and future possibilities accordingly rather than consider the potential validity of other, different interpretations or points of view. Gabriel often interprets his life in biblical terms. For example, he believes that God, not he, is the agent behind his love for Elizabeth as well as for Deborah (his first wife): " 'Sister Elizabeth,' he said, 'the Lord's been speaking to my heart, and I believe it's His will that you and me should be a man and wife' " (187). Similarly, Gabriel believes that the first Royal's death is not his fault – he interprets it either as God's will or as Esther's fault: "Her curse [('bastard')] had devoured the first Royal; he had been begotten in sin, and he had perished in sin; it was God's punishment, and it was just" (114). He refuses any alternative interpretations of these events – that, for example, the first Royal's death might be partly due to Gabriel's irresponsibility toward Esther and his refusal to acknowledge his son.

Gabriel imposes a religious paradigm on his life experiences because he wants to avoid, at any expense, feeling fragmented and the responsibility he would have to take for his actions if he allowed himself to realize that his "Christian" acts (such as beating the "sin" out of John) were of his own volition. On another occasion, Gabriel again refuses responsibility by interpreting Roy's street-fighting injury as the fault of white boys:

"You see?" came from his father. "It was white folks, some of them white folks *you* like so much that tried to cut your brother's throat." John thought, with immediate anger and with a curious contempt for his father's inexactness, that only a blind man, however white, could possibly have been aiming at Roy's throat; and his mother said with a calm insistence: "And he was trying to cut theirs." (45–46)

Gabriel avoids responsibility for Roy's actions (and thereby allows Roy off the hook as well) by forcing his interpretation to fit under the paradigm of the evil of white people. He desires certainty and unity so much that he is willing to misinterpret life experiences in order to avoid any uncertainty about himself.

The fact, however, that many characters continue to feel split or fragmented and see events in their lives as disparate and not unifiable suggests that a unity of experience and a coherent, nonfragmented self or identity are not really attainable, despite the desire. John desperately wants to achieve a continuity of self and time, and he believes that the church can offer this:

Tonight, his mind was awash with visions: nothing remained. He was ill with doubt and searching. He longed for a light that would teach him, forever and forever, and beyond all question, the way to go; for a power that would bind him, forever and forever, and beyond all crying to the love of God. . . . And his mind could not contain the terrible stretch of time that united twelve men fishing by the shores of Galilee, and black men weeping on their knees tonight, and he, a witness. (80)

Yet within the same paragraph, the narrator tells us that the "fury and anguish [that] filled him" were "unbearable, unanswerable," suggesting that John's desire cannot be fulfilled. Baldwin makes this message more concrete at the end of the novel because even after John is "saved," he still has feelings of fragmentation: "Yet, as he moved among them . . . something began to knock in that listening, astonished, newborn, and fragile heart of his; something recalling the terrors of the night, which were not finished, his heart seemed to say; which, in this company, were now to begin" (206). The "terrors of the night" to which he alludes include his feeling that he was "something that had no power of itself, any more, to turn" (193) because "the utter darkness does not present any point of departure, contains no beginning, and no end" (194).

Baldwin thus clearly points to the impossibility of a unified self because, apart from John, even a character as blindly absolute as Gabriel has momentary doubts about whether his attempts to unify his life experiences are in fact valid. Yet even when Gabriel exhibits self-confidence and arrogance (when he has no uncertainty), we remain skeptical about his holy interpretations of his actions due to the cognitive and narrative dissonance that we confront as readers. When other preachers make fun of Deborah's asexual piety at a church dinner (before Gabriel even contemplates marrying her), Gabriel hotly defends her as his "sister in the Lord" (108). Because Baldwin reveals Gabriel's egocentric thoughts a few sentences later, however, we, as readers, are unsure whether Gabriel defends Deborah's honor because he cares about her or because he needs to feel superior to others. There is an ironic disjuncture between how he acts and what he thinks: "they went back to their eating and drinking, as though the matter were finished. Yet Gabriel felt that he had surprised them; he had found them out and they were a little ashamed and confounded *before his purity.* And he understood suddenly the words of Christ, where it was written: 'Many are called but few are chosen' " (108, emphasis added). Because Gabriel's motives are unclear to us (although they seem to be very clear to him) – perhaps he acts out of pride, one-upmanship, chivalry, piety, or purity – we sense an ironic gap (cognitive ambivalence) in Baldwin's narration. We also doubt Gabriel's purity because we see him through other characters' eyes. For example, the recollections of Florence (Gabriel's sister) and Gabriel of childhood events are quite different. Thus through direct and indirect ambivalence, Baldwin conveys that on many levels apparent unity is just that: apparent only. Therefore, narrative dissonance and cognitive ambivalence function not only within the novel, but without it as well, with readers. Baldwin enacts a kind of layered interwoven ambivalence: Characters have inner doubts or feelings of dislocation, they see gaps in the apparent seamlessness of others' lives, and, finally, we as readers sense ambivalence in places that the novel's characters may not.

But cognitive ambivalence also has to do with each subject's multiple layers of identity; different components of a subject's identity can conflict. For example, when her husband Frank comes home after an argument, Florence is caught between her sexual desire for Frank (heterosexual femininity) and her prideful urge to control and be better than Frank (what she sees as her class status – as being above what she calls "ragtag" and "dirty" "common niggers" [85]), which she could exercise by refusing his sexual advances; "And this caused such a war in her as could scarcely be endured. She felt that everything in existence between them was part of a mighty plan for her humiliation. She did not want his touch, and yet she did: she burned with longing and froze with rage" (87). Because Baldwin leaves textual contradictions intact, he implies that aspects of identity and the roles attached to them are provisional, mutable, and multivalent: The relative importance of different aspects of identity is not fixed because Baldwin refuses to transfix his characters in a hierarchical notion of identity wherein, for example, gender would always be more important when considering Florence than would be race, class, or sexuality. Obviously, when one considers Florence in different contexts (as a daughter, as a wage-worker, as an aunt, as a wife, as a minister's sister, as a single woman, as a black woman in a rural or urban setting), various ingredients of her identity are not separable, but their interactions may compute differently according to context.

In other words, Baldwin explores an interactive "multiplicative" conceptualization of identity rather than an additive one. In an incremental analysis of identity, the relationships among constituents of identity as well as among types of discrimination are simplified and unified along single axes and it is often presumed that subject positions such as "woman," "man," "black," "heterosexual," and "Christian" are therefore monolithic, distinct, and separable. A multiplicative analysis of identity does not presume that "one factor can and should supplant the other. . . . The modifier 'multiple' refers not only to several, simultaneous oppressions but to the multiplicative relationships among them as well" (King 80–82). Like contemporary black gay filmmaker Marlon Riggs, Baldwin avoids ranking identities and issues in a hierarchy of relevance or importance: Riggs wants

> to show the multiplicity of our conditions within the black community and how we deal with issues of sexuality and race, gender, class, political consciousness, political responsibility, and identity. Identity is a big issue. As some would phrase it: "What are we first . . . ?" I try to invalidate that argument. Part of the message . . . is to realize that you are many things within one person. Don't try to arrange a hierarchy of things. (Simmons 191)

Thus, although characters in the novel may be unable to do so, Baldwin asks his readers to contemplate fragmented, multilayered, and unresolved narrative accounts in order to consider the value in recognizing that we are many things at once and that to "arrange a hierarchy" of our identities is to deny the fluidity of our subjectivity. Deconstructing single, stable identities that cross time and space does not suggest that we do not have identities: We do; but these identities are flexible and result from an array of interrelated conditions (Roof, *Lure*, 158).

Because Baldwin's characters do not have identities that are fixed or absolute, he is able to portray many different features of human identity with sympathy and equanimity. Fluctuating and mutable identities act as a means of understanding other people's positions, both for Baldwin and for the reader. Baldwin's female characters are complex and empathic because knowledge does not have to follow from being, ontology does not necessarily precede epistemology: Baldwin does not have to *be* a heterosexual black woman in order to portray one well. In order to have empathy, however, Baldwin has to attempt to de-center those elements of his identity that could obscure his understanding – he must not let being a man, for example, hinder his pursuit of portraying multidimensional black womanhood. Baldwin's many-layered rendering of multivalent identities requires a certain humility and a belief that to identify with someone's position does not require sameness, does not necessitate a parallel, synonymous subjectivity. Baldwin's fragmented and discordant narrative structure therefore forces his readers also to adopt a certain humility, to de-center, at times, parts of their identities in order to focus on the multilayered narration of events at hand. Through Baldwin's narrative, readers come to understand that in Elizabeth's life, for instance, social constructions of womanhood, race, and heterosexuality[1] all converge and influence her life's decisions, are related to the ways in which she sees herself, and to how others view her. Elizabeth is complex, not unidimensional. In addition, Baldwin's exploration of the mutability of subjectivity and of social roles affords him empathy toward social issues not directly linked to his identity. Domestic violence (for example, Gabriel beating Elizabeth as well as Roy and John) and interracial rape (for example, Deborah's teenage trauma) are portrayed as equally problematic, traumatic, and worthy of focus as black male on male violence in the streets (for example, the two Roys) and the lynching of black men (for example, the soldier on the outskirts of town) by white men.

Portraying the subjectivity of his characters as fragmented allows Baldwin to critique white society as well as the black community from within. He identifies concerns often overlooked by many black men (such as domestic violence – supposedly a "women's" or "children's" issue in conventional juridico-political analyses wherein issues are tied to so-called genetic factors such as gender and race) that are connected to the multiple oppressions black women face.[2] This is not to say that Baldwin does not focus keenly on the negative and harmful effects that a pervasive whiteness has on the characters in the novel. Whiteness, as a prevalent cultural construct, makes sporadic yet detrimental appearances in the novel, whether through the characters' imagination or through direct interracial conflict. For example, both Florence's and Elizabeth's conceptions of beauty are influenced by a racialized gender ideology in which white femininity and bodies are considered to be more beautiful and desirable – by the dominant white culture and by some members of the black community. Florence imagines that her dark skin makes her unattractive:

> She stared at her face in the mirror, thinking angrily that all these skin creams were a waste of money, they never did any good. . . . [Frank asked her,] "Is you coming to bed, old lady? Don't know why you keep wasting all your time and *my* money on all them old skin whiteners. You as black now as you was the day you were born." "You wasn't there the day I was born. And I know you don't want a coal-black woman." "I ain't never said nothing like that. You just kindly turn out that light and I'll make you to know that black's a mighty pretty color." (88, 90)

Elizabeth's conflict with beauty and skin color comes earlier in her life. As a child, Elizabeth connects her mother's lack of affection for, and interaction with her to the disparity in skin color between herself and her mother: "it was, perhaps, her mother's disquieting color that, whenever she was held in her mother's arms, made Elizabeth think of milk. Her mother did not, however, hold Elizabeth in her arms very often. Elizabeth very quickly suspected that this was because she was so very much darker than her mother and not nearly, *of course*, so beautiful" (153, emphasis added). Baldwin's probing of the self-conceptions of these two women, and their understanding of beauty, clearly demonstrates that there is a "cycle between representation and reality" (Julien and Mercer 171) wherein fictional constructs of gendered racial ideology become "true." For example, Florence using skin whiteners is simultaneously a reaction to and a reinforcement of a culturally created belief that whiteness is more beautiful and feminine than blackness. By exploring the definitions of these two female characters of what is beautiful, Baldwin not only shows how oppressive constructs are internalized by the victims of those constructs as "true," but he also demonstrates that notions of beauty and desire are established within the myriad interconnections between racial, sexual, and gender ideologies.

Baldwin reveals the overvaluation of whiteness to be an achievement and not a given fact, but he also indirectly upholds blackness as beautiful. For instance, the milky complexion of Elizabeth's mother is "disquieting." Moreover, the comments of Florence's husband Frank clearly evoke his desire for and appreciation of Florence. Similarly, although Elizabeth experiences discomfort and distancing from her mother due to her darker skin color, her father believes that Elizabeth *is* beautiful: "He told her that she was the apple of his eye. . . . When she was with her father she pranced and postured like a very queen. . . . And he was dark, like Elizabeth, and gentle, and proud" (153). Thus, through the words and actions of men important in Florence's and Elizabeth's lives, Baldwin upholds darkness as beautiful while simultaneously exposing the harms of racialized gender ideologies. Baldwin undercuts racialized gender constructions at the same time that he invokes them. His critique lies simultaneously within and outside of the black community. He criticizes racism (external – defining blackness as unfeminine, as undesirable) as well as internalization and perpetuation (internal – buying skin creams). Baldwin emphasizes that ideologies rarely completely subjugate people. Simultaneous oppression and resistance are most evident when Elizabeth comes in contact with the police officers who want to question her about Richard:

> She moved between them, out into the sun. She knew that there was nothing to be gained by talking to them any more. She was entirely in their power; she would have to think faster than they could think; she would have to contain her fear and her hatred, and find out what could be done. . . . [S]he kept her head high, looking straight ahead, and felt the skin settle over her bones as though she were wearing a mask. (161)

Obviously, Elizabeth is *not* "entirely in their power." She just appears to be. She succumbs to their dominance to the extent that she obediently comes with them, between them, down to the station. She plays the part of the docile black female. She simultaneously rejects their control of her, however, because she immediately starts to wonder how to outsmart them – which she knows she can do, if she is careful.

Aside from enacting a simultaneous internal-external critique, Baldwin's presentation of many-layered changeable identities and narrative constructions also focuses on how sexuality, desire, and gender are as socially and linguistically embedded as is race. Therefore, Baldwin explores how an aspect of identity such as masculinity is something learned, a "reaction formation," and not a given or "originary model of selfhood" (Di Stefano 46). The beating Gabriel gives John after John looks at his father's penis in the bath reinforces the idea that in order to be a (heterosexual) "man," John should not sexualize the male body. John *learns* to think of such transgressive thoughts as "sinful" – the masculine identity he is in the process of exploring is formed, in part, in reaction to the results of his probing the definitional parameters of "manhood." Most "Christian tradition, following Paul, holds that sex is inherently sinful. It may be redeemed if performed within marriage for procreative purposes and if the pleasurable aspects are not enjoyed too much" (Rubin 11). Because John learns that sexuality is considered negative and destructive, his sexualizing of his father's body is doubly transgressive: He violates conventional definitions of heterosexual masculinity and crosses over the line between sanctified (heterosexual) reproductive sexuality into sexuality as pleasure and desire. Through John's transgressions, Baldwin indirectly portrays how fundamental the church has been in defining and controlling sexuality (Edwards 17). Baldwin demonstrates that social and cultural pressures affect how we pursue and acquire the trappings of identity. Masculine and feminine identities are learned and acquired, not stable; they are tentative.

Masculinity and femininity change not only according to social and cultural contexts, but also in concurrence and interaction with other components of identity (for example, hetero/homosexuality, Christianity, fatherhood/motherhood, blackness). When Elizabeth leaves home and goes to New York with Richard, she finds that part of what she took to be "inherently" feminine was, in fact, a learned characteristic that she quickly unlearns:

> [S]he found occasion to wonder, ruefully, what had made her imagine that, once with Richard, she would have been able to withstand him. She had kept, precariously enough, what her aunt referred to as her pearl without price while she had been with Richard down home. This, which she had taken as witness to her own feminine moral strength, had been due to nothing more, it now developed, than her great fear of her aunt, and the lack, in that small town, of opportunity. (162)

In other words, the tentativeness of our identities is related to their multiplicative and changeable nature. Elizabeth's thoughts on her sexuality also show how "proper" and appropriate identity roles are often the result of compulsory control (Butler, "Imitation," 313).

Thus racial, sexual, and gender constructions can all be seen as discursive ideologies which regulate people's actions, and not as presocial or inherent givens. Baldwin explores how subjects are not necessarily formed through self-conscious actions or by self-assertion. In the novel, gender, race, and sexuality are "embedded in linguistic structures which are self-replicating and which give meaning to . . . difference"; identities are grounded in socio-linguistic constructions, but these productions do not radically determine the subject (Cornell 98; 139). For example, the abundance of biblical terminology in the novel underscores how features of our identities are not only learned, but are reinforced and given meaning through words. On the first page, Baldwin conveys that John's (future) identity as a preacher is constructed and reinforced through spoken language: "Everyone had always said that John would be a preacher when he grew up, just like his father. . . . It had been said so often that John . . . had come to believe it himself. Not until the morning of his fourteenth birthday did he really begin to think about it, and by then it was too late" (11). His religious identity as a preacher also intersects with the formation of both his masculine identity, because preaching is a traditionally masculine role, and his (supposed) sexual identity, for being a preacher portends heterosexual marriage and fatherhood. Baldwin more directly conveys that masculinity, heterosexuality, and being a preacher all interconnect when Gabriel recalls his conversion: "And this was the beginning of his life as a man. . . . He moved into town . . . and he began to preach. He married Deborah in that same year. . . . [B]ecause there was no one, any more, to look after him, she invited him often to her home for meals, and kept his clothes neat, and after he had preached they discussed his sermons; that is, he listened while she praised" (98).

A few pages after Baldwin introduces the idea that it is too late for John to question his oft-mentioned future identity, we see more explicitly how (biblical) language not only constructs, but reinforces and gives meaning to identity attributes and their accompanying appropriate roles:

> His father's face, always awful, became more awful now; his father's daily anger was transformed into prophetic wrath. His mother, her eyes raised to heaven, hands arced before her, moving, made real for John that patience, that endurance, that long suffering, which he had read of in the Bible and found so hard to imagine. . . . On Sunday mornings the women all seemed patient, all the men seemed mighty. (15)

In the context of biblical language, gender roles – masculinity and femininity – are rendered indubitable. Because John considers the men and women on Sundays through a lens he adopts from things he has "read of in the Bible," he understands men to be, and become, strong or "mighty," whereas he interprets the women's strength as "patient" and "long-suffering." Just as Florence's use of skin creams makes real the racialized constructions of beauty, so do Elizabeth's actions make real for John traditional oppositional gender roles; Baldwin again emphasizes the interconnections between representation and reality.

Thus, the myriad layers of identity take place in the context of other discourses such as racism and sexism, but also in and through the matrix of language. Discursive practices do not radically determine the subject, however, even though they constitute the subject. The distinction lies in the fact that, for example, John is – or will be – uncertain about his identity as a preacher. Although he is rocketing toward the threshing floor, and despite Baldwin's implication that his future as a preacher is inevitable (for doubting comes "too late"), because John has second thoughts about and will continue to question his religious identity (and all that it implies about manhood) his subjectivity is not determined to the extent that he is unable to think outside himself. John's wavering conveys that although his identity is constructed through words, cultural and familial expectations, and gender ideology, he is able to deconstruct that identity: Identity constructions are not absolute.

Baldwin invokes tensions between narrative representations

to underscore how features of identity (such as masculinity) appear to be imporous and seamless because of the dynamics of representation. Representation is simultaneously real and illusory. Representations are "true" in that they replicate and perpetuate the world in their own images, hence John's ability to see gender identities through a biblical lens. But representations are also illusory because they violate and do injustice to the "realities" they represent. Crystalline coherent gender, racial, and/or sexual identities result from the repetition of an apparently contiguous sameness of identity (Butler, "Imitation," 314). However, when there are gaps or breaks in that repetition (such as Elizabeth's "loss" of her feminine sexual purity), the continuity and stability of an identity are revealed to be performative, not inherent. By unmasking seamlessness as an effect and not a fact, Baldwin underscores how all identities are constituted through action and how none is completely coherent.

In other words, to have an identity is always to enact a kind of masquerade or approximation of that identity. The subject and the psyche, the conscious and the unconscious, being and knowledge are no longer conflated. John senses that people cannot really "be" outside of discursive contexts, that "being" is a kind of mirage: "John . . . saw them for a moment like figures on a screen, an effect that the yellow light intensified. . . . Through a storm of tears that did not reach his eyes, he stared at the yellow room; and the room shifted, the light of the sun darkened, and his mother's face changed" (21, 22). But Baldwin explores approximate masquerade more concretely at other points in the novel. For instance, Gabriel puts on a masculinity to which he knows the women at the bar will react: He "drank again, allowing, unconsciously, or nearly, his face to fall into the lines of innocence and power which his experience with women had told him made their love come down" (95). The women John observes on the street in the first pages of the novel are not conventionally feminine because they "fought *like* the men" they are with (12, emphasis added). These women adopt masculine characteristics when it suits their purposes. Baldwin illustrates that gender roles do not have to follow from biology; to "be" a female does not mean that one has to "be" feminine. Femininity is something that can be shed or taken up, depending on context. In this vein Roy and John imitate masculine and feminine roles in the process of mocking each other: " 'Oh, I *beg* your pardon,' said Roy, in the shrill, little-girl tone he knew John hated. 'What's the *matter* with you today?' John asked, angry, and trying at the same time to lend his voice as husky a pitch as possible" (23). Baldwin, by repeating the theme that identities are mutable, parodic performances, reinforces their temporary, momentary, and tentative qualities (Dhairyam 28). Moreover, because characters shed their "true" identities in order to perform *like* other identities, Baldwin reveals that representing identity involves exclusion. To "be" feminine, Roy does not use the lower registers of his vocal chords, whereas to "be" masculine, John employs his husky tones to their fullest capacity. The disparity between a character's "true" and "adopted" identities reveals that the "true" identity is also a masquerade, a performance which emphasizes certain characteristics and downplays others.

Thus ambivalence stemming from narrative dissonance is connected to the discrepancies between representations of identity in the novel; they both function to underscore "the violence implicit in the process of representation itself" (Tucker 91). Baldwin explores the violence of representation by illustrating how characters in the novel are relational – how they define and differentiate themselves in relation to each other. For example, Gabriel realizes that he needs Deborah as a wife to accentuate his identity as a pious, righteous minister and that she needs him to define her as a desirable and whole woman. Having been raped by white men as a teenager excludes her from being considered a desirable woman – she can only be seen as either a pitiful victim or a lustful whore. Because she is caught in a virgin-whore oppositional paradigm, Deborah can only achieve an (illegitimate) sexual identity through a performative approximation of a harlot: "she might, with ironic gusto, have acted out that rape in the fields forever" (73). Baldwin demonstrates that Gabriel's sexual past does not haunt him in the same way because of a sexual double standard: "Again, there was her legend, her history, which would have been enough, even had she not been so wholly unattractive, to put her forever beyond the gates of any honorable man's desire" (98). Gabriel indirectly defines who he is as an "honorable man" when he imagines who Deborah is. He fixes her identity as an undesirable yet pious woman and excludes or circumnavigates other facets of her identity in order to make his own identity concrete:

> For she sustained him most beautifully in his new condition; with her unquestioning faith in God, and her faith in him, she, even more than the sinners who came crying to the altar after he had preached, bore earthly witness to his calling; and speaking, as it were, in the speech of men she lent reality to the mighty work that the Lord had appointed to Gabriel's hands. . . . [A]s the Lord had given him Deborah, to help him to stand, so the Lord had sent him to her, to raise her up, to release her from that dishonor which was hers in the eyes of men. (99, 109)

Baldwin deconstructs this "relational concept of difference" by revealing its reliance on dominating and violating the Other who occupies the opposite "side" of such self-definitions. Baldwin underscores, through all the characters, but most obviously in one such as Gabriel, that a "relational concept of difference falters precisely when it projects the Other as conceptualized only in relation to me. In other words, it tames the otherness of the Other by making her mine" (Cornell 171). Gabriel's egocentrism when imagining Deborah shows how imagining and representing another human being involves reducing the layers of her or his identity. Defining one's self in opposition entails freezing the Other in a frame of reference and minimizing that person's changeability. Because Gabriel is narcissistic and wants to control and have power over others, he decontextualizes those around him more than someone like John who recognizes and struggles with his fragmentation. Imagining and representing others in relation to one's self at center not only transfixes those others in a miniaturization, it also attempts to solidify the self at center as coherent, unchangeable, and seamless. Yet, paradoxically, the tranquil surface of representation is ruptured by the violence to the other which that smoothness attempts to cover over – by narrative and cognitive dissonance. Thus Baldwin explores the ways in which a subject defines her- or himself and is defined by others through differentiation and decontextualization. Social constructs form the present but unacknowledged process behind a subject's production (Butler, "Contingent," 12). The exclusions necessary to invoke unified subjectivity do, however, return to haunt Baldwin's characters, to disrupt their claims to coherence through diverse forms of narrative and cognitive ambiguity.

Ambivalence, invoked by conflicting memories, self-doubting, a sense of incoherence or instability, and gaps that lie between different narrative strands, points to those aspects of a character's identity that "escape or resist administration, regulation, . . . expression" (Honig 226) and conscious identification. Narrative irresolution also signifies that there is an excess to one's subjectivity which one can never fully know: John

> attacked the mirror with the cloth, watching his face appear as out of a cloud. . . . He stared at his face as though it were, as indeed it soon appeared to be, the face of a stranger, a stranger who held secrets that John could never know. And, having thought of it as a face of a stranger, he tried to look at it as a stranger might, and tried to discover what other people saw. But he saw only details. . . . These details did not help him, for the principle of their unity was undiscoverable, and he could not tell what he most passionately desired to know: whether his face was ugly or not. (27)

This passage emphasizes that a desire for unity cannot erase fragmentation or alienation. Moreover, because John cannot arrange the "details" in the mirror signifies that a ranking of identity characteristics is neither possible nor useful in pursuing self-knowledge. The passage also underscores how full knowledge of self is impossible – that there is a psychological excess or a beyond to the conscious self which cannot be regulated, much less discovered or identified.

The rhetorical layers of the novel not only function, therefore, on the level of the consciously stated, but also as the "trope of the unsaid" (Hutcheon 82). Thus much of the novel's ambivalence is conveyed not only by Baldwin juxtaposing disparate points of view, but also by his utilizing implied narrative to explore ideas deemed unthinkable or invisible. John's sexuality is not manifestly homosexual. It is eclipsed because "if one does not have an overt sexual identity in a society where heterosexuality is omnipresent, one essentially passes as heterosexual" (Edwards 54). His indeterminate sexual identity is not only lost from view to others, however. His passing is both interior, in his own mind, as well as exterior – he is an invisible man to himself and others. Although John's homosexual desire[3] is equivocal, this does not suggest that there is a hidden "true," unified coherent homosexual self which, once revealed, will end John's search for coherence. Baldwin's narrative suggests that homosexual desire will be among many coefficient variables of John's subjectivity – it will continue to function as a factor in his multiplicative identity. John's subjectivity, like that of other characters in the novel, will continue to be an illusion of wholeness which his subconscious excess, beyond control of the knowing self, will continually undermine. One's selfhood can never be fully unveiled. Baldwin's multifold narrative structure allows homosexual desire to be conveyed without being explicitly delineated: Homosexual desire is embedded in the novel's discontinuity – in and between the layers of the text just as it lies in and between the layers of John's conscious self. Therefore, ambivalence also demonstrates that

> oppression works not merely through acts of overt prohibition, but covertly, through the constitution of viable subjects and through the corollary constitution of a domain of unviable (un)subjects – *abjects*, we might call them – who are neither named nor prohibited within the economy of the law. Here oppression works through the production of a domain of unthinkability and unnameability. (Butler, "Imitation," 312)

John cannot *be* gay because the gay subject *is not*. To be gay is not viable for John because the option does not exist within his frames of reference – gayness is never mentioned once in the novel.

That Baldwin never names homosexuality in the novel does not imply John is not homosexual. Rather, it conveys that John cannot consciously enact that subject position and it allows Baldwin to avoid the paradox of representation he explores throughout the novel: He circumscribes the "paradoxical containment of the uncontainable" (Roof, "Lesbians and Lyotard," 51). Homosexuality lies beyond John's conscious realm because it is deemed unthinkable: It is a pariah position, not a subject position. Thus through dissonance, the unnameable outside a character's realm of consciousness arises anyhow – John's sense of fragmentation signifies a beyond to his knowing self. Baldwin's consistent use of ambivalence in the novel not only signifies that identities are mutable and provisional, but also that the gaps, malaise, and "ill-fittedness" can be "sites of critical leverage" (Honig 231). Moreover, Baldwin infers that an outsider position is slippery – "that the pariah is itself unstable, that the pariah is never really an outsider, and that its sites are multiple" (Honig 232). John is simultaneously an insider and an outsider – he has religious and homosexual desire. Therefore, Baldwin refuses to place John on either side of an oppositional paradigm. John oscillates between multiple sites of identity – he is not fixed in one location.

Ambivalence also prompts the reader to question the possibility for, and desirability of, transcendence – both religious or secular-political. Because Baldwin contests religious, racial, sexual, and gendered discourses from within, he implies that one cannot completely escape the parameters of discursive practices even though discursive practices are not all-encompassing. Baldwin's deconstruction from within avoids an oppositional paradigm that would reinvoke dynamics he works to transgress. If he attempted to speak from "outside" – from a blackness that was never hurt by white domination – he could risk reifying dominant central discourse. He could therefore replicate the kinds of representations of the "real" and "true" that he wants to avoid.

Baldwin unmasks essentialist and dichotomous premises of religionist, racist, sexist, and heterosexist discourses by simultaneously enacting and parodying their conceptual oppositions, which was clear in his internal-external critique of racialized conceptions of beauty. Baldwin's exploration of the performative and approximate nature of human identities also shows a continuum between masculinity and femininity rather than a mutually exclusive opposition. The two other oppositions that Baldwin deconstructs at length are the sinner-saved and the heterosexual desire-unnameable/homosexual desire oppositions. Baldwin invokes dichotomies only to show them in flux, to show, for example, Gabriel's constant (but not necessarily conscious) oscillation between the carnal and the spiritual, being a sinner and being saved, rather than his clearly occupying one "side" of the opposition. Gabriel believes that such an opposition is possible. He clearly demarcates between his (former) life of sin and his (present) spiritual life. Anything reminiscent of his carnal existence is simply a remnant of the past – it has no place, in his mind, in his present:

> This silence, continuing like a corridor, carried Gabriel back to the silence that had preceded his birth in Christ. Like a birth indeed, all that had come before this moment was wrapped in darkness, lay at the bottom of the sea of forgetfulness, and was now counted against him, but was related only to that blind, and doomed, and stinking corruption he had been before he was redeemed. (92)

Readers see this dichotomy as false: Gabriel's evil ways continue on into his redeemed life. The "saved" Gabriel takes joy in Florence's humility in church: "She knew that Gabriel rejoiced, not that her humility might lead her to grace, but only that some private anguish had brought her low: her song revealed that she was suffering, and this her brother was glad to see. This had always been his spirit. Nothing had ever changed it; nothing ever would" (65). The "Christian" Gabriel also blames his abandonment of the now-dead first Royal and of Royal's mother, Esther, on his wife Deborah: " 'I asked my God to forgive me,' he said. 'But I didn't want no harlot's son.' 'Esther weren't no harlot,' she said quietly. 'She weren't my wife. I couldn't make her my wife. I already had *you*' – and he said the last words with a venom" (148). And Gabriel blames the second Royal's bad activities either on white people (as discussed earlier) or on his second wife Elizabeth:

> "I'm out of this house," he shouted, "every day the Lord sends, working to put the food in these three children's mouths. Don't you think I got a right to ask the mother of these children to look after them and see that they don't break their necks before I get back home?" "You ain't got but one child," she said, "that's liable to go out and break his neck, and that's Roy, and you know it." . . . They stared at each other a moment

in an awful pause, she with a startled, pleading question in her eyes. Then, with all his might, he reached out and slapped her across the face. She crumpled at once. (47–48)

Gabriel's belief in oppositional dichotomies allows him to avoid responsibility for his actions and in-depth self-examination. The sinner-saved paradigm allows him to conclude that, because he is saved, problems in his life such as poverty, domestic violence, and "unruly" children must be caused by other "sinners" – Elizabeth for example. Because, for the reader, the sinner-saved dichotomy is so obviously untrue in Gabriel's life, Baldwin indirectly shows oppositions to be fluid and unstable forms of representation which rely on false notions of fixed identity locations, obscuring how dichotomies are "mutable fabrications" (Tucker 92).

Baldwin interrogates the supposed opposition between heterosexual and homosexual desire through John's imagination. John sometimes imagines homosexuality by invoking images of heterosexuality. This suggests that sexuality is a continuum, not an either/or paradigm. On his birthday morning, John's imagination wanders from a conventional sexualization of the female body into an eroticization of male bodies. John

stared at a yellow stain on the ceiling just above his head. . . . ; and then (while the yellow stain on the ceiling slowly transformed itself into a woman's nakedness) he remembered that . . . he had sinned. . . . He had sinned. . . . [H]e had sinned with his hands a sin that was hard to forgive. In the school lavatory, alone, *thinking of the boys, older, bigger, braver,* who made bets with each other as to whose urine could arch higher, he had watched in himself a transformation of which he would never dare to speak. (18–19, emphasis added)

John uses conventional heterosexual imagery of female nakedness to recall masturbation and an erection in the school washroom which occurs while he is thinking about the "manlier" boys' penises arcing urine. Because homosexuality is unnamed and invisible in the text and in John's mind, he displaces homoeroticism through conventional heteroerotic imagery – the only sexual imagery he knows of. This sexualization of masculinity is subversive in that images of masculinity are not supposed to be sexually objectified by men (Edwards 50).

Thus John transmutes an apparently nonsexual context – the lavatory – into an erotic one. John makes other apparently nonsexual situations homoerotic as well – especially Elisha's actions in the church. Such contextual transgressions can be considered important signifiers of homosexual desire because, for example, eroticizing Elisha allows John an outlet for homoerotic desire that does not disrupt perceptions of heterosexual normality. John maintains an outward appearance of "normalcy" while simultaneously (but not necessarily consciously) playing out his desires. On the third page of the novel, we learn that John is

> distracted by his new teacher, Elisha. . . . John stared at Elisha all during the lesson, admiring the timbre of Elisha's voice, much deeper and manlier than his own, admiring the leanness, and grace, and strength, and darkness of Elisha in his Sunday suit, wondering if he would ever be holy as Elisha was holy. But he did not follow the lesson, and when, sometimes, Elisha paused to ask John a question, John was ashamed and confused, feeling the palms of his hands become wet and his heart pound like a hammer. (13)

Baldwin again interweaves manliness and holiness, suggesting that the masculinity that John learns is constructed in and through Christianity. Baldwin also moves his readers into slowly seeing Elisha as John sees him: We, too, see Elisha's attractive body and actions, we hear his appealing voice. The eroticization of Elisha is more evocative a few pages later when the narrator describes John watching Elisha. Unlike the more subtle sexual references in the first description (sweaty palms, pounding heart), this second erotic transgression is much more overt:

> John watched. . . . And then Elisha danced. At one moment, head thrown back, eyes closed, sweat standing on his brow, he sat at the piano, singing and playing; and then, like a great, black cat in trouble in the jungle, he stiffened and trembled, and cried out. *Jesus, Jesus, oh Lord Jesus!* . . . Then he was on his feet, turning, blind, his face congested, contorted with this rage, and the muscles leaping and swelling in his long, dark neck. It seemed that he could not breathe, that his body

could not contain this passion. . . . His hands, rigid to the very fingertips, moved outward and back against his hips, his sightless eyes looked upward, and he began to dance. Then his hands closed into fists, and his head snapped downward . . . ; his thighs moved terribly against the cloth of his suit. . . . and then, in a moment, with a cry, head up, arms high in the air, sweat pouring from his forehead, and all his body dancing as though it would never stop. Sometimes he did not stop until he fell . . . moaning, on his face. (15–16)

Through John's watching, Baldwin eroticizes Elisha for the reader: the reader, in the act of reading, replicates John's eroticization and contextual transgression. Baldwin leads the reader into seeing and enacting homoeroticism from within. The multiple layers of the text (wherein erotic imagery is embedded) force readers to occupy, in the act of reading, a subject position that does not overtly exist in the novel. Through homoerotic imagery, readers come to "see" the invisible even though John cannot: "He wanted to stop and turn to Elisha, and tell him . . . something for which he found no words. . . . John, staring at Elisha, struggled to tell him something more – struggled to say – all that could never be said" (219–220). Homoeroticism also underscores how, for John, (homo)sexuality and the church are inextricably intertwined. The church indirectly allows John access to homosexual desire at the same time that (homo)sexuality is proscribed. Thus the church, ironically, also has a mutable function. Like changeable and approximate human identities, the church is also not a stable institution. It, too, is always in the process of becoming and of risking destabilization, even though it appears to be coherent.

The institution of the church functions ironically for other characters in the novel as well. The church offers Gabriel a sanctified arena for his will to power: "he wanted power – he wanted to know himself to be the Lord's anointed, His well-beloved. . . . He wanted to be master, to speak with that authority which could only come from God" (94). Not only does the church offer him an outlet for mastery, but he uses its doctrines to justify his abusive acts (such as beating Roy, John, and Elizabeth). Gabriel also eroticizes domination and submission of women through the lens of religion. Lust, conquest, and epiphany are interconnected for him from the moment of his "redemption." His thoughts were still on his activities with the (anonymous) woman of the night before – "in vanity and the pride of conquest, he thought of her, of her smell, the heat of her body beneath his hands, of her voice, and her tongue" (96) – when he comes to a rise in the hill and is born again. His eroticization of sexual and religious submission surfaces later when, trying to convert Esther, Gabriel "imagined her, because of the sermon that he would preach, *on her knees* before the altar" (118, emphasis added). At first, readers may consider that Esther is on her knees to pray, but we soon see that it is submission to him, not to God, that Gabriel desires: "Having *possessed* Esther, the carnal man awoke, seeing the possibility of *conquest* everywhere" (127–128, emphasis added). The church offers Gabriel a chance to foster his egocentric vanity and to justify his vengeance toward others.

The church offers Florence little. Florence, too, likes to be in control, but the church offers her, as a woman, no outlet for this desire. Florence recalls that of all her mother's prayers for the protection of her children, there was only one "in which her mother demanded the protection of God more passionately for her daughter than she demanded it for her son" (68). The church's and her mother's overvaluation of masculinity meant that there "was only one future in that house, and it was Gabriel's" (72). Florence is denied food, clothing, attention, and an education – all because she is a daughter, not a son. Gabriel's and Florence's roles in the church are gendered: Religious roles intertwine with gender roles. Thus not only does the church not offer Florence an outlet – it works against her.

The only socially sanctioned outlet that Florence has for power is marriage, so she tries to control Frank – his dress, manners, friends, and activities – "And this had given her, in the beginning of their marriage, the impression that she controlled him. This impression had been entirely and disastrously false" (82). The conventional (heterosexual) masculine role of provider and protector is ill-fitting for Frank: "[H]e had never made enough money to buy the home she wanted, or anything else she really wanted" (84). Florence's wants are socially constructed – she expects certain things from a marriage and a man because that is the way it is "supposed" to be. Baldwin again underscores the paradoxical cyclical relation between representation and reality. Florence defines Frank in opposition to her; by delineating his faults, Florence also defines who she is in relation to him.[4] Frank often plays up this opposition to suggest its limits: " 'And what kind of man you think you married?' 'I thought I married a man with some get up and go to him, who didn't just want to stay on the bottom all his life!' 'And what you want me to do, Florence? You want me to turn white?' " (85). At other times, Frank turns the "sides" of the opposition around. Florence complains, " 'You reckon I slave in this house like I do so you and them common niggers can sit here every afternoon throwing ashes all over the floor?' 'And who's common now, Florence?' he asked, quietly, in the immediate and awful silence in which she recognized her error" (85). Florence's fixation on class mobility and the heterosexual provider role Frank should fulfill demonizes Frank – she can only see him in these contexts. Eventually, Frank plays his "lack" to the fullest – he parodies her dichotomy most – when he leaves for good. " 'All right, baby, I guess you don't never want to see me no more, not a miserable, black sinner like me.' The door closed behind him, and she heard his feet echoing down the long hall, away" (82). Florence's upbringing, wherein she is denied an active role in church and the community because of socially prescribed gender roles, also limits her adulthood. Because of her preconceptions, Florence futilely struggles to have power over Frank, to rein him in – she tries to fulfill her sanctioned role as a Christian woman.

The role of the church seems different for Elizabeth. She believes that it can offer her some things she wants: safety and honor. Because of Christian heterosexual conventions, Elizabeth believes that her sexual relations with Richard and their illegitimate son John – "Elizabeth's shame" (152) – make her a fallen woman. When young, Elizabeth seems able to see behind social conventions: She sensed "that what her aunt spoke of as love was something else – a bribe, a threat, an indecent will to power" (156). Yet when she meets Gabriel, she ignores her inner thoughts for what he, symbolizing the church and conventional

heterosexuality, could offer her; "his eyes had made her know that she could be again – this time in honor – a woman" (184). Elizabeth passively allows Gabriel to define who she is – she buys into traditional heterosexual relations: "Gabriel had become her strength. . . . [H]er safety lay before her, like a hiding-place hewn in the side of the mountain" (186). It is not that she did not sense Gabriel's urge for power early on, nor that she does not know this later. When she first meets him, "she looked into his eyes [and] found a strange humility, an altogether unexpected kindness. She felt the anger go out of her, and her defensive pride; but somewhere, crouching, the fear remained" (182). In the present, Elizabeth thinks that "he cherished her – *if* he cherished her – only because she was the mother of his son, Roy. All of this she had through the painful years divined" (175). Through her body Elizabeth rescues and reproduces Gabriel's patriarchy by giving him the son he wants and by allowing him to beat her: her body and self-effacement serve Gabriel's will to power.

Elizabeth overlooks Gabriel's yearning for mastery and her role in maintaining it because she believes that he saved her from falling further into destruction. If she had followed her father's advice, Elizabeth might never have married Gabriel, and she surely never would have stayed: "It was he who had told her to weep, when she wept, alone; never to let the world see, *never to ask for mercy;* if one had to die, to go ahead and die, but *never let oneself be beaten*" (154, emphasis added). Because of Christian paradigms, Elizabeth can only see her own actions as truly sinful, for Gabriel's are excused due to his sanctioned role as preacher.

> [S]he thought of Richard. . . . Not even tonight . . . could she wish that she had not known him; or deny that, so long as he was there, the rejoicing of Heaven could have meant nothing to her – that, being forced to choose between Richard and God, she could only . . . have turned away from God. And this was why God had taken him from her. It was for all of this that she was paying now. (157)

Elizabeth denies other possible interpretations of her life events. The church functions as a foil; it is impossible for her to consider that racism killed Richard and that her fall was not in loving Richard, but in succumbing to marriage to Gabriel. The church offers her limited agency, for God is all-powerful – the creator and destroyer of life. Elizabeth gets so caught up in the web of dichotomous religious paradigms – good/evil, God/Devil, sinner/saved, leader/follower – that she cannot think her way out.

Baldwin's portrayal of the function of the church as ironically mutable is linked to his exploration of the approximate, tentative, and multiplicative nature of human identity. He explores the violence of representation and the cycle between representation and reality through his characters' interdependence on each other as well as through their bonds to the structure of the church. Both reality and subjectivity are unstable yet interconnected in and through their constructedness. Baldwin shows his characters as caught up in linguistic and visual representations of reality that are self-replicating but not all-encompassing. The church's representations of reality are powerful, but they cannot completely dominate: Homoeroticism leaks in and through the layers of the text; Gabriel's will to power is exposed as such; Elizabeth cannot deny her love for Richard; and Florence, in leaving home, refuses to be held back by limiting roles. Through discord and ambivalence, Baldwin conveys a many-sided interpretation of a reality that is always, through tensions, subversions, and ill-fitting replications, in the process of becoming.

NOTES

1 Sexuality, like gender and race, is not presocial. Like other parts of human identity, it is forged in and through social, historical, and linguistic contexts and constructs. Ideas about sexuality and about what is "normal" and "deviant" change across time and space. As David Halperin puts it, "Sexuality is not a somatic fact; it is a cultural effect" ("Is There a History of Sexuality?" *The Lesbian and Gay Studies Reader* [New York: Routledge, 1993], p. 416). Heterosexuality is the presumed "normal" sexuality in our culture: its normalcy is reinforced through obscenity and deviancy laws, medicine, psychiatry, scripture, and even marriage laws, insurance poli-

cies, and "family values" debates. Part of the semantic merging of biology with desire is due to the fact that, in English, "sex" means both (Gayle Rubin, "Thinking Sex," *The Lesbian and Gay Studies Reader*, p. 32). In addition, because heterosexuality's normalcy is reinforced at so many levels of our society, it is also compulsory, but its compulsoriness is hidden by its apparent natural normalcy: Heterosexuality can be considered an ideology like those of race and gender because it is self-perpetuating and its dynamics are not readily apparent, but are embedded in the ways in which our daily lives are structured.

2 For further exploration of this issue, one of the first black feminist anthologies is particularly helpful: See *The Black Woman: An Anthology*, edited by Toni Cade Bambara (New York: Mentor, 1970).

3 Using the possessive (i.e., John*'s* homosexual desire) is problematic in the context of Baldwin's use of indeterminacy as it relates to identity. My naming John *as* homosexual or as *having* homosexual desire fixes and contains John's identity in a way that Baldwin does not. In other words, the possessive implies a transparency and knowability of human identity and it violates Baldwin's textual irresolution and ambivalence. Baldwin forecloses absoluteness and certainty via indeterminacy, but naming John as (definitively) homosexual forecloses the play of Baldwin's text: therefore, I only use the possessive case sparingly when considering John's sexual desires.

4 As discussed earlier, in the case of Gabriel and Deborah this kind of oppositional relational way of seeing others violates the complexity of human identity in that it fixates both people in a dichotomy and it limits the play between identity traits through miniaturization and decontextualization.

WORKS CITED

Baldwin, James. *Go Tell It on the Mountain*. New York: Dell Publishers, 1981 (1953).

Butler, Judith. "Contingent Foundations: Feminism and the Question of 'Postmodernism.' " In Butler and Scott, eds., *Feminists Theorize the Political*. New York and London: Routledge, 1992, pp. 3–21.

"Imitation and Gender Insubordination." In Abelove, Barale, and Halperin, eds., *The Lesbian and Gay Studies Reader*. New York and London: Routledge, 1993, pp. 307–320.

Cornell, Drucilla. *The Philosophy of the Limit.* New York: Routledge, 1992.

Di Stefano, Christine. *Configurations of Masculinity: A Feminist Perspective on Modern Political Theory.* Ithaca and London: Cornell University Press, 1991.

Dhairyam, Sagri. "Racing the Lesbian, Dodging White Critics." In Laura Doan, ed., *The Lesbian Postmodern.* New York: Columbia University Press, 1994.

Edwards, Tim. *Erotics and Politics: Gay Male Sexuality, Masculinity, and Feminism.* New York and London: Routledge, 1994.

Honig, B. "Toward an Agonistic Feminism: Hannah Arendt and the Politics of Identity." In Butler and Scott, *Feminists Theorize the Political,* pp. 215–235.

Hutcheon, Linda. *Splitting Images: Contemporary Canadian Ironies.* Toronto and Oxford: Oxford University Press, 1991.

Julien, Isaac and Kobena Mercer. "True Confessions: A Discourse on Images of Black Male Sexuality." In Essex Hemphill, ed., *Brother to Brother: New Writings by Black Gay Men.* Boston: Alyson Press, 1991, pp. 167–173.

King, Deborah K. "Multiple Jeopardy, Multiple Consciousness: The Context of a Black Feminist Ideology." In Malson, O'Barr, Westphal-Wihl and Wyer, eds., *Feminist Theory in Practice and Process.* Chicago and London: Chicago University Press, 1989, pp. 75–106.

Roof, Judith. "Lesbians and Lyotard: Legitimation and the Politics of the Name." In Doan, *The Lesbian Postmodern,* pp. 47–66.

A Lure of Knowledge: Lesbian Sexuality and Theory. New York: Columbia University Press, 1991.

Rubin, Gayle S. "Thinking Sex: Notes for a Radical Theory of the Politics of Sexuality." In Abelove, et al., eds., *The Lesbian and Gay Studies Reader,* pp. 3–44.

Simmons, Ron. "*Tongues Untied:* An Interview with Marlon Riggs." In Hemphill, ed., *Brother to Brother,* pp. 189–199.

Tucker, Marcia. "Mechanisms of Exclusion and Relation: Identity." In Ferguson, Olander, Tucker, and Fiss, eds., *Discourses: Conversations in Postmodern Art and Culture.* Cambridge: MIT Press, 1990, pp. 91–92.

6

Baldwin, Communitas, and the Black Masculinist Tradition

KEITH CLARK

> No. I've never seen one [a community of writers] in any case . . . and I don't think any writer ever has.
>
> Interview with Jordan Elgrably and George Plimpton, 1984

> Many articles in the house caught my attention, most notably the many paintings and pieces of sculpture, among them the colorful paintings of the late African-American expatriate painter Beauford Delaney, who had been one of Jimmy's best friends. There were two other pieces that I believed said very much about the political commitment of the man. One, a black pen-and-ink drawing of Nelson Mandela against an orange background, accompanied by a poem, was framed and hung over the dining-room fireplace, the most prominent place in the house. The other was an assemblage created by Jimmy's brother David in his honor.
>
> Quincy Troupe, "Last Testament: An Interview with James Baldwin," 1988

IN evaluating and situating James Baldwin's career and life, one encounters several complexities and paradoxes; not coincidentally, the word "conundrum" recurs in his writings and interviews. As a writer whose life and art reflected so many conflicting and sometimes binary oppositions – Europe/America, heterosexual/homosexual, political/personal, black/white, male/female, art/protest – he experienced conflicts as an isolated artist who simultaneously craved community. The epigraphic quotations attest to Baldwin's "divided" self, one that would reject the idea of "literary" community, but whose personal living space would render a cosmic link among an eclectic group of black men: artists, politicians, and blood brothers.

One cannot read Baldwin's oeuvre without situating him within a tradition of black masculinist writers. If one motif binds

texts such as Douglass's *Narrative of the Life of Frederick Douglass, an American Slave Written by Himself* (1845), James Weldon Johnson's *Autobiography of an Ex-Coloured Man* (1912), Richard Wright's *Black Boy* (1945), and Ralph Ellison's *Invisible Man* (1952), it is the quest for wholeness in a society where the black self is, in Houston Baker's words, "under erasure" (Baker, *Blues Ideology*, 153). I contend that although Baldwin is connected inextricably to the black masculinist canon, he nevertheless traversed the discursive framework of his literary brothers and keepers; certainly, "Baldwin's aesthetics represent a new departure" (Baker, *Journey Back*, 61). Baldwin's place in a literary male communitas is unequivocal but problematic, for his works attempted to counter limiting constructions of the black male self. Ultimately, I see a tenuous and ambiguous relationship between Baldwin and his literary brothers, reflected in his inscription of black men's relationships in his autobiographical novel, *Go Tell It on the Mountain*.

Baldwin and Black Masculinist Discourse: Toward a (Re)definition of the Black Male Subject

Before beginning a discussion of Baldwin's prophetic and wrenching first novel, I believe that it is imperative to offer a critical/theoretical framework for his writings. The author's own comments about his most tortured protagonist, jazz musician Rufus Scott from the novel *Another Country* (1962), reveal his reconceptualization of the male subject:

> A lot of people in that book had never appeared in fiction before. People overlook this fact. And there's an awful lot of my experience which has never been seen in the English language before. Rufus, for example. There are no antecedents for him. He was in the novel because I didn't think anyone had ever watched the disintegration of a black boy from that particular point of view. Rufus was partly responsible for his doom, and in presenting him as partly responsible, I was attempting to break out of the whole sentimental image of the afflicted nigger driven that way (to suicide) by white people. (Standley and Pratt 104)

Baldwin posits Rufus's unique place in the black literary landscape while signifying on the "Wright school," a black literary tradition which falls under the rubric of American "naturalism."[1] The allusion to "black boy" is quite significant, for Baldwin radically critiqued and reconfigured the Wrightian protagonist, one shaped exclusively by a hostile, sterile environment.

Without question, Richard Wright remains the father of black "protest," the sine qua non in any discussion of literature's responsibility to agitate and propagandize. That his name remains synonymous with protest fiction recalls what Michel Foucault posits in his essay "What Is an Author?":

> Finally, the author's name characterizes a particular manner of existence of discourse. Discourse that possesses an author's name is not to be immediately consumed and forgotten; neither is it accorded the momentary attention given to ordinary, fleeting words. Rather, its status and its manner of reception are regulated by the culture in which it circulates. (Foucault, *Critical Theory,* 142)

Clearly, Wrightian protest represented a benchmark for Baldwin's own aesthetics, for Wright represented the towering fatherly presence that he "slew" in essays such as "Many Thousands Gone" and "Alas, Poor Richard." But what transpires here is more than a mere Freudian struggle in which neophyte writer metaphorically kills his literary father, a menacing figure who must be exorcised in order to secure his own literary space. Baldwin vehemently repudiates the protest tradition, the Wrightian discourse that articulated the black man's victimization at the hands of an impenetrable white society – the discourse which, to alter Foucault's lexicon, could consume and regulate Baldwin's own voice.

Codifying protest discourse can be a slippery slope, for as novelist Ann Petry has said, "The novel, like all other forms of art, will always reflect the political, economic, and social structure of the period in which it was created" (Petry 33). Nevertheless, Wright's work is the apogee of black masculinist protest discourse, evinced by his novel *Native Son* (1940) and his autobiography *Black Boy.* Indisputably, Wright's work impacted and shaped myriad authors, from Chester Himes to Petry to John A. Williams. More than any author, he captured the abject victimization of the black male and white America's complicity in his destruction.

Returning for a moment to Foucault, I borrow his concept "discursive formation" as a referent for Wrightian protest: "Whenever one can describe, between a number of statements, such a system of dispersion, whenever, between objects, types of statement, concepts, or thematic choices, one can define a regularity (an order, correlations, positions and functionings, transformations), we will say . . . that we are dealing with a *discursive formation*" (Foucault, *Archaeology,* 38; emphasis in original). Rufus Scott thus represented a departure from the discursive formation of Wrightian protest; Baldwin was concerned not so much with how white society de-formed and destroyed the black self, but how this self conspired in his own demise. With *Go Tell It on the Mountain,* Baldwin entered and interrupted a protest discourse which inscribed the black man's physical and mental erasure fait accompli, without delving into the formation of this black male subject; he rejects the discursive relationship between protagonist and author in which the former merely embodies otherness and difference.

Indeed, Baldwin began a reconstruction and reconfiguration of the black male subject. The author's own critique of *Native Son* informs his aesthetic aims, providing the contours of his critical/theoretical position:

> What the novel reflects – and at no point interprets – is the isolation of the Negro within his own group and the resulting fury of impatient scorn. It is this which creates its climate of anarchy and unmotivated and unapprehended disaster; and it is this climate, common to most Negro protest novels, which has led us all to believe that in Negro life there exists no tradition, no field of manners, no possibility of ritual or intercourse, such as may, for example, sustain the Jew even after he has left his father's house. (*Notes of a Native Son* 35–36)

Baldwin laments Wright's erasure of the black community, his disregard for entities and structures that have allowed black folks to "get over" – be they family, church, civic clubs, fraternities, or sororities. Baldwin's critical project has thus been the reconstruction of whites' conception of blackness as signifying absence and difference. Baldwin's critique of Wright recalls Ellison's comments about white conceptualizations of the black subject: "In the Anglo-Saxon branch of American folklore and in the entertainment industry . . . the Negro is reduced to a negative sign that usually appears in a comedy of the grotesque and the unacceptable" (Ellison, *Shadow and Act,* 48). The tradition of *Native Son,* with the "grotesque" Bigger Thomas as the incarnation of black subject as "negative sign," catalyzes and informs Baldwin's refiguration and re-centering of the black male as both *de-formed* and *de-centered* subject: one who exists on the margins of not only white society, but of his native black community as well.

When I speak of the black male subject as de-centered, I am not merely invoking a postmodernist conceptualization of subjectivity, what Peter Middleton calls a "kind of subjectivity-less subject: interpellated by ideology, constructed by discourses, constituted by the desire of the other" (Middleton 117). One could read Bigger as the archetypal de-centered subject, as he is unequivocally constructed based on Wright's political ideologies and defined by disparaging discourses which demonize blackness. But *Go Tell It on the Mountain* also inaugurates a reconception of voice in black masculinist literature. Critics such as Horace Porter have elaborated on the link between Baldwin and psychological realists such as Henry James, who introduced the free indirect method of constructing narrative; Baldwin himself acknowledges James's influence: "There were things I couldn't deal with technically at first. . . . This is where reading Henry James helped me, with his whole idea about the center of consciousness and using a single intelligence to tell the story. He gave me the idea to make the novel happen on John's [Grimes] birthday" (Standley and Pratt 238).[2] But Baldwin's narrative strategy is more complex than this.

Although John Grimes represents the initial point of view and reference, Baldwin demonstrates his concern with communitas by saturating the text with multiple voices in the forms of the three "Prayers" which constitute the second section of the novel. In addition, his characters hear a plethora of "voices" which influence and control their (re)telling of their lives; this is especially evident during Gabriel's prayer and John's conversion on the "threshing-floor." Baldwin thus de-centers his narrative in that he inscribes a chorus of voices, a narrative strategy that distinguishes him from both Wright and Ellison. Baldwin's conceptualization of voice is reminiscent of Russian formalist critic M. M. Bakhtin's narratological position: "The novel as a whole is a phenomenon multiform in style and variform in speech and voice. In it the investigator is confronted with several heterogeneous stylistic unities, often located on different linguistic levels and subject to different stylistic controls" (Bakhtin 261). Clearly, Baldwin complicates the notion of voice; the proleptic *Go Tell It on the Mountain* anticipates works such as Ernest Gaines's *A Gathering of Old Men* (1983), where the author conflates voice, communitas, and black male subjectivity.

Though Baldwin's "moral and imaginative geography lie[s] well beyond the social realism or naturalism championed by Wright" (Dixon 124), this aesthetic departure is somewhat tenuous and at times problematic. Baldwin's ardent repudiation of Wrightian discourse is more than a little reminiscent of what Harold Bloom calls the "anxiety of influence." Like Wright and Ellison, Baldwin not only adopted white literary role models, but he expressed an anxiety about blackness as well. Remembering his sojourn in Switzerland (with friend Lucien Happersberger), he admits:

> Well, that winter in Switzerland, I was working on my first novel – I thought I would never be able to finish it – and I finally realized that one of the reasons that I couldn't finish this novel was that I was ashamed of the Blues, ashamed of Jazz, and, of course, ashamed of watermelon: all of these stereotypes that the country inflicts on Negroes, . . . When I say I was trying to dig back to the way I myself must have spoken when I was little, I realized that I had acquired so many affectations, had told myself so many lies, that I really had buried myself beneath a whole fantastic image of myself which wasn't mine, but white people's image of me. (Standley and Pratt 4)

This anxiety is central to my discussion of *Go Tell It on the Mountain*. From a textual standpoint, Baldwin's admission, along with his comments about the centrality of James, demonstrates a centering of white literary modes and models. Not only does James's ghost haunt the narrative, but the similarities between Baldwin's bildungsroman and James Joyce's *Portrait of the Artist as a Young Man* are unequivocal.

I believe these white "intertexts" complicate Baldwin's staunch repudiation of Wrightian protest discourse. Obviously, Wright's work is informed by the naturalist/protest writers of the late nineteenth and early twentieth centuries (Balzac, Dreiser, and others). And though Baldwin distinguishes his text through its narratological design, he does mimic Wright in a larger literary discursive context: He too relies on "already written" narrative paradigms about religious, adolescent, familial, and sexual conflicts. This ontological dialectic – represented by the textual presences of Joyce and James – reflects Baldwin's reliance on what Bakhtin calls "authoritative discourse":

> The authoritative word demands that we acknowledge it, that we make it our own; it binds us, quite independent of any power it might have to persuade us internally; we encounter it with its authority already fused to it. The authoritative word is located in a distanced zone, organically connected with a past that is felt to be hierarchically higher. It is, so to speak, the word of the fathers. Its authority was already *acknowledged* in the past. It is a *prior* discourse. (Bakhtin 342; emphasis in original)

Baldwin appears to privilege a modernist discourse which is the accepted literary apparatus. This does not mean that he does not imbue the text with what I will later discuss as a black blues voice, but it does suggest a desire to situate himself within a context of "authorized," hegemonic writers.

The conflicted artistic space which Baldwin inhabits – among white modernists and the black protest writer, his literary fathers – surfaces in *Go Tell It on the Mountain* as well. This "paradox of communitas" forms the basis for my reading of relationships between the book's male figures. Though Michel Fabre is quite correct in asserting that it "plays with a constellation of fathers – unknown and mythical father, real and legitimate father, putative father, possible father, adulterous husband and father of a bastard" (Fabre, "Fathers and Sons," 124), the novel traverses consanguineous relationships; there exists a "constellation" of interlocking male relationships, binding John, Gabriel, Elisha, and Richard, as well as "minor" characters such as Florence's husband, Frank. Part of Baldwin's own "rejection" of blackness debilitates John and Gabriel, both of whom are ill prepared for black male intimacy and emulate the practices of a white male power structure.

Baldwin's De-formed Disciples and the Paradoxical Search for Communitas

In Karen Thorsen's documentary *James Baldwin: The Price of the Ticket,* Maya Angelou eloquently remarks that *Another Country* is about people "trying desperately to love each other." Though critics often focus on the antagonistic relationships between fathers and sons, I feel her comment informs *Go Tell It on the Mountain.* Obviously, women play a central role in the narrative, but as in all his works, Baldwin centers men's relationships and the price they pay in attempting to forge connections. Ultimately, the novel depicts men at varying stages of communitas. The central trinity – John, Gabriel, and Elisha – reflects the different phases; it might be helpful to recall Jean Toomer's *Cane* (1923) in conceptualizing these three characters. Toomer begins with the southern "thesis," shifts to the northern "antithesis," and reconciles these oppositions in the concluding Kabnis section, the "synthesis." Vis-à-vis this schema, John represents "thesis," Gabriel "antithesis," and Elisha "synthesis." Baldwin ultimately depicts men on the *threshold* of communitas; these chimeric images of communitas are evident in brief tableaux – blues moments when the men cast aside their conflicting and constricting precepts regarding their value as black men.

John maintains the most conflicted position of the male characters. Baldwin "centers" him only in that his perspective opens and closes the novel, bracketing the other characters' voices and remembrances of things past. Clearly, John is relegated to the margins, as the text abounds with instances where he desires male recognition. He engages in a Herculean struggle with both his father and stepbrother Roy, both of whom dehumanize John in different ways; two of these episodes are particularly resonant. The first involves John's literal and metaphorical "reflection." As he cleans a mirror, he gazes at himself hauntingly:

> Thinking bitterly of his birthday, he attacked the *mirror* with the cloth, watching his face appear as out of a cloud. With a shock he saw that his face had not changed, that the hand of Satan was as yet invisible. *His father had always said that his face was the face of Satan* – and was there not something – in the lift of the eyebrow, in the way his rough hair formed a V on his brow – that *bore witness to his father's words?* . . . But he saw only details: two great eyes, and a broad, low forehead, and the triangle of his nose, and his *enormous mouth,* and the barely perceptible cleft in his chin, which was, his father said, the mark of the devil's little finger. These details did not help him, for the principle of their unity was undiscoverable, and he could not tell what he most passionately desired to know: whether his face was ugly or not. (27, emphasis added)

Baldwin raises several salient issues regarding John's conception of himself and his relationships with other men. The fact that he is housecleaning marks the beginning of a "gender problem" which burdens him repeatedly; this might explain the difficulty he experiences in becoming a "gendered subject."[3] Johnny's self-portrait is the antithesis of the Lacanian "mirror stage," which Terry Eagleton summarizes: "The child, who is still physically uncoordinated, finds reflected back to itself in the mirror a gratifyingly unified image of itself; and although its relation to this image is still of an 'imaginary' kind . . . it has begun the process of constructing a centre of self" (Eagleton 164). What John perceives is not a "unified image," but a fragmented and disembodied self – a physically de-formed one. Moreover, John's "centre of self" is mediated by his father's gaze, Gabriel's gross misreading of John's body. This moment of self-reflection recalls Henry Louis Gates's "trope of the talking book," where slave Olaudah Equiano attempts to speak to a book, having watched his master reading. But when he gazes at and listens to the book, it does not "talk back," for Equiano as object is relegated to silence: "Only a subject [his master] can speak. Two mirrors [himself and the book, two "objects"] can only reflect each other, in an endless pattern of voided repetition" (Gates 156).

John's textualized self – a "voided" one he reads through his father's harsh assessments – brands him as "evil" and foreshadows Gabriel's use of religion as a weapon; in addition, John's unequivocally "black" features cast him in a foreboding, liminal space he inhabits throughout his entire life – a world that views blackness as alien ("ugly") and one that privileges whiteness. John will hopelessly hold himself up to the mirrors of race and gender and will always find himself horribly disfigured and deformed. His "enormous mouth" is especially ironic, for John, like his father (and Baldwin), will crave *voice* and *audience* – a community of black men to "bear witness," to validate and embrace him. His voicelessness and emasculation coalesce when Roy mocks him "in the shrill, little-girl tone he knew he hated" (23). Finally, John's marginality and silence transcend the bounds of family, as he can only "witness" visually the boys' ritual of stickball:

> The cold sun made their faces like copper and brass, and through the closed window John heard their coarse, irreverent voices. And he wanted to be one of them, playing in the streets, unfrightened, moving with such grace and power, but he knew this could not be. Yet, if he could not play their games, he could do something they could not do; he was able, as one of his teachers said, to think. But this brought him little in the way of consolation, for today he was terrified of his thoughts. He wanted to be with these boys in the street, heedless and thoughtless, wearing out his treacherous and bewildering body. (30)

John envisions himself as part of an adolescent fraternity of black boys who aren't silenced or ostracized. His ability to think – his imprisonment in an asphyxiating interior reality – is the legacy of his father Richard, a suicide who also found himself lacking an outlet for his blues.

Relegated to the periphery of the adolescent male communitas, John fashions an alternative world resplendent with books and movies. His longing for community emerges on his fourteenth birthday, which only his mother remembers. He embarks on a journey with the money she has given him, venturing from Broadway to the public library to the movie house. It is interesting that he first encounters a white man in a scene which revises the beginning of *Invisible Man*. When John starts to apologize for almost knocking down the old man, "the old man smiled. John smiled back. It was as though he and the old man had between them a great secret; and the old man moved on" (34–35). This foreshadows John's immersion in a white world, emblematized by the movie house, where he further associates himself with white popular culture. First,

> He stopped at last before a gigantic, colored poster that represented a wicked woman, half undressed, leaning in a doorway, apparently quarreling with a blond man who stared wretchedly into the street. The legend above their heads was: "There's a fool like him in every family – and a woman next door to take him over!" He decided to see this, for he identified with the blond young man, the fool of his family, and he wished to know about his so blatantly unkind fate. (37)

John re(con)textualizes himself in terms of both white patriarchal and popular culture to counter his abjectly bleak black universe; if he must be a member of the sullied "Grimes" family, he can at least camouflage his blackness and begin to transform himself into a white blond male, the apogee of privilege and power in American society.

Once inside the theater, the dynamics of John's gender "confusion" are reified when he identifies with the film's white female protagonist:

> He wanted to be like her, only more powerful, more thorough, and more cruel; to make those around him, all who hurt him, suffer as she made the student [the white blond male] suffer, and laugh in their faces when they asked for pity for their pain. *He* would have asked no pity, and his pain was greater than theirs. Go on, girl, he whispered, as the student, facing her implacable ill will, sighed and wept. Go on, girl. One day he would talk like that, he would face them and tell them how much he hated them, how they had made him suffer, how he would pay them back! (39; emphasis in original)

John's reconceptualization of himself as white male *and* female illuminates a psychologically frayed black male subject who desperately seeks voice and audience. His "response" to the film is especially poignant and tragic, for it conveys his own voicelessness and powerlessness. John is reduced to a negative sign, one who must look not only outside his race but outside his gender for voice and authority. But there is no antiphonal call and response between him and the film's protagonists; neither the white man nor woman will answer him. John's aborted speech act – his hollow "go on, girl" – is as futile and unsatisfying as his masturbating (about which he feels perpetual guilt). He exists as pure object who can only attach himself to the sound and fury of whites who are oblivious to his culture and existence. The author himself was acutely aware of the black adolescent's misdirected hero(ine) worship: "You go to the white movies and, like everybody else, you fall in love with Joan Crawford, and you root for the Good Guys who are killing off the Indians. It comes as a great psychological collision when you realize all of these things are really metaphors for your oppression, and will lead you into a kind of psychological warfare in which you may perish" (Standley and Pratt 5).

John's sequestration of himself into a hermetically sealed world of books and movies is a legacy he comes by honestly. His father, Richard, bequeaths to his "bastard" son a passive, "artistic" self who exists in an epistemological prison. Whereas John seeks refuge in the public library, Richard visits New York's museums. He, too, found in education a weapon he thought would retrieve him from the margins.[4] Responding to Elizabeth's query about his hunger for knowledge, he confesses:

> I just decided me one day that I was going to get to know everything them white bastards knew, and I was going to get to know it better than them, so could no white son-of-a-bitch *nowhere* never talk *me* down, and never make me feel like I was dirt, when I could read him the alphabet, back, front, and sideways. (167)

Significantly, Richard makes this observation in New York City, for which he fled Maryland; thus, his northern pilgrimage and quest for literacy recall the life of Douglass. But the plethora of negative words, as well as the thematically resonant "dirt" reference, convey Richard's miseducation – his attempts to earn the recognition of whites through literacy. On the other hand, he spends time gazing at African cultural artifacts during his museum excursions; as John's ancestor, he, too, desired a communal kinship with his own people. But Richard's quest is problematic in the same way that John's recreated self is: He privileges and centers a dominant white culture and looks to it for validation, albeit in the guise of black militancy.

Moreover, he fails to realize that his attempts to gain a white audience to listen to his "talk" are ill–conceived, as ill–conceived as his son's subsequent attempts to locate his voice through white movie heroines. Richard will never be able to wash away the "dirt" that he allows whites to heap on his psyche; therefore, he forges a cosmic bond with his son, whose name evokes the same omnipresent filth. As Trudier Harris points out, "Richard's intellectual ability to deal with the world is not matched by an equally strong emotional ability" (Harris 52), and his subsequent suicide bespeaks his vitiated attempt to dismantle the master's house with the master's language. Richard's internalization of whites' dehumanizing conception of blackness provokes his self-destruction: Once the white policeman who wrongly jails him spews "You black bastards . . . you're all the same," Richard's futile attempt to reconstruct himself in terms that whites will acknowledge is exposed, and he slits his wrists while alone in his apartment – a narrow, confining tomb (note that Richard was imprisoned in "The Tombs," an infamous New York prison) as sepulchral as John's movie house.

Bloodlines engender links between John and Richard, but Gabriel Grimes maintains a central presence as a black male subject who sabotages his unmet desire for communitas. Though readers and critics often vilify Gabriel as John's tormentor and the martinetlike head of the Grimes household, he nevertheless – albeit intermittently – expresses a need to formulate some sort of blood male communitas. Only when he begins to exploit religion to secure voice and authority does he experience the self-erasure and marginalization that befell John's natural father and Gabriel's "unnatural" stepson.

For instance, Gabriel's relationship with his biological son, Roy, illuminates a nurturing, responsive Gabriel. During the stabbing episode, he "muttered sweet, delirious things to Roy, and his hands, when he dipped them again in the basin and wrung out the cloth, were trembling" (42). This ritual father-son baptismal is replicated, as John recalls "Communion Sunday":

> They knelt before each other, woman before woman, and man before man, and washed and dried each other's feet. Brother Elisha had knelt before John's father. When the service was over they had kissed each other with a holy kiss. (56)

Obviously, the homoerotic undertones of this episode provide John a vicarious physical connection. But these scenes also present a different Gabriel, a "prelapsarian" one who had not yet appropriated religion/Christianity as an instrument of domination.

Just as Richard's exodus from the South brought neither wholeness nor connection, Gabriel's emigration is less than fulfilling; contrarily, it brings a concomitant loss of audience and status: "His father no longer, as he had once done, led great revival meetings, his name printed large on placards that advertised the coming of a man of God" (50). The erasure of Gabriel's name – his deinscribing – is compounded by an accompanying silencing as well, for he functions as an ersatz minister in Harlem's "Temple of the Fire Baptized": "Rarely did he bring the message on a Sunday morning; only if there was no one else to speak was his [John's] father called upon. He was a kind of fill-in speaker, a holy handyman" (51). Unlike that of antecedents such as Douglass, his geographic relocation brings silence.

Gabriel's loss of status, reified in his ministerial voicelessness, is especially debilitating considering his ardent desire for the voice and authority which he had realized in the South:

> Yes, he wanted *power* – he wanted to know himself to be the Lord's anointed, His well-beloved, and worthy, nearly, of that *snow-white* dove which had been sent down from Heaven to testify that Jesus was the Son of God. He wanted to be *master, to speak with that authority which could only come from God.* (94, emphasis added)

This passage is salient for a number of reasons. Foremost, it reveals Gabriel's association with a male dominated, omnipotent religion; as God's ambassador, he can traverse the narrow parameters imposed by both blacks (such as the preachers at the "Twenty-Four Elders Revival Meeting") and white men (such as those responsible for raping his first wife, Deborah, and those who kill a black soldier recently returned from war). Second, the often-cited color symbolism is significant as well; for Gabriel "Christ is a kind of spiritual bleaching cream" (Bone 223). Words such as "snow-white" and "master" illustrate how Gabriel suffers from the same self-hatred that prostrate Richard and John, the same quest for white power and approbation that the black man can never hope to attain. Cultural critic bell hooks insightfully historicizes the black male subject's loss of identity and his appropriation of white configurations of masculinity as a result of his geographic re- and dis-location:

> Certainly, in the mass migration from the rural south to the urban north, black men lost status. In southern black communities there were many avenues for obtaining communal respect. A man was not respected solely because he could work, make money, and provide. The extent to which a given black man absorbed white society's notion of manhood likely determined the extent of his bitterness and despair that white supremacy continually blocked his access to the patriarchal ideal. (hooks 91)

Indeed, Gabriel has absorbed a white patriarchal ideology which poisons his relationships with other blacks. Baldwin reveals one portentous piece of the Grimes family history in the section "Florence's Prayer." Rachel, Gabriel and Florence's mother, was born into slavery and underwent its attendant horrors – most notably, the seizure of her own children to be sold at auction and sexual violation by her white master (69–70). This history of male domination becomes Gabriel's *ur-text*, the one into which he (re)situates himself.

Gabriel first attempts to seduce Esther with his voice, inviting her to an evening service to hear him preach; ironically, Deborah's scripture about "a man of unclean lips" had prefaced his sermon for the "Twenty-Four Elders Revival Meeting." Though Esther fails to respond to his perverted "call," she and Gabriel eventually "fall": "he and Esther in the white folks' kitchen, the light burning, the door half-open, grappling and burning beside the sink" (126); minutes earlier Gabriel had seen Esther drinking the "master's whiskey" (124). After their brief but torrid relationship, Gabriel achieves a discursive symbiosis of sorts, synthesizing the ideology of white American men concerning slavery and the Judeo-Christian mythology about the inherent evil of women.

First, Gabriel disposes of Esther and their son in the same way that many slaveowners ridded themselves of their unwanted slave mistresses and their illegitimate offspring. Baldwin invokes these historical practices by having Gabriel fund Esther's flight to the north. Tragically, Chicago functions for Esther as it did for her literary predecessor, Bigger Thomas – as a figurative and spiritual tomb, for she dies after the birth of Royal. Just as slaveowners decreed that "the children of the slave women shall in all cases follow the condition of their mothers" (as Douglass lamented his own dispossession [Douglass 49]), Gabriel never acknowledges his "bastard": He repudiates both mother and son, whom he considers abominations.

In addition to the "white codes" he invokes to dispose of his unwanted "family," Gabriel arrogates another Foucaultian "discursive fact" – this one involving the omnipresent biblical declarations of the frailty and wantonness of women. Eve, Jezebel, Mary Magdalene – the Bible abounds with women who are synonymous with iniquity. Gabriel recasts himself as the "fallen" Adam, a Dimmesdalean victim of the "temptress" Esther ("Hesther"). Responses such as "I ain't the first man to fall on account of a wicked woman" and "But I didn't want no harlot's son" demonstrate a reckless disregard for his own complicity in his "fall." Although there is some validity to Harris's suggestion that "Esther dies and Gabriel thrives" (Harris 49), Gabriel, like Satan, is consigned to the hell of himself. By privileging a framework which at one time sanctioned slavery as "God's will" (the myth of Ham is one of Baldwin's biblical intertexts), Gabriel belies his own history as an oppressed other by recreating himself as a *faux* white man.

Finally, Gabriel's Sutpenian quest for a "royal line" of heirs – a sacrosanct male communitas – represents his final thwarted search for (comm)unity. He models himself after biblical heroes such as Abraham and David, thereby mimicking an Anglo-

Christian ethos of male hegemony. He myopically fails to see his "misappropriations," however; in fact, the wayward sons of his biblical "fathers" often remained estranged. As H. Nigel Thomas adduces, "Because Gabriel is trapped in his Old Testament beliefs, God's 'unfulfilled promise' leaves him a hateful man who victimizes his household with his guilt-derived anger" (Thomas 149). Although Baldwin's third-person narrator concludes that "there was no word in the Book for him" (136), this phrase could be read literally as well as figuratively. Gabriel attempts to textualize himself via a biblical discourse which upholds patriarchy and male privilege, unwilling to acknowledge how his position as black male subject complicates his reading of the "Word" – a text he misreads and misuses as a basis for his own aborted attempts to conceive a "royal line."

Thus, Gabriel's de-centering of black culture and community in his unfulfilled quest for voice and authority represents an unashamed privileging of the values of others – most notably belief systems that have historically been inimical to African-Americans. René Girard in *Deceit, Desire, and the Novel: Self and Other in Literary Structure* constructs a paradigm he calls the *mediator of desire,* which helps elucidate Baldwin's narrative schematization. He posits that "triangular" desire exists when a subject "imitates" the desires of a more privileged "other":

> Don Quixote, in Cervantes' novel, is a typical example of the victim of triangular desire, but he is far from being the only one. Next to him the most affected is his squire, Sancho Panza. Some of Sancho's desires are not imitated, for example, those aroused by the sight of a piece of cheese or a goatskin of wine. But Sancho has other ambitions besides filling his stomach. Ever since he has been with Don Quixote he has been dreaming of an "island" of which he would be governor, and he wants the title of duchess for his daughter. These desires do not come spontaneously to a simple man like Sancho. It is Don Quixote who has put them into his head. (Girard 3)

Girard's example is apropos, for it illustrates how the agon at the center of Cervantes' classic also surfaces in Baldwin's classic text. Just as Sancho mimics Don Quixote in craving power and authority, so too do Gabriel and, to a lesser degree, John, allow the terms of intimacy to be defined by others.

Gabriel's exploitation of Esther and preoccupation with biblical stories about bloodlines and male progeny represent his own form of mediated desire. Esther, for instance, in and of herself holds little "value" for Gabriel; only as someone at the bottom of the race-gender hierarchy does she assume any worth. Appropriately enough, Gabriel's lust is heightened after he sees Esther sneaking the "master's whiskey." Thus, when he takes her in the "white folks' kitchen," Gabriel replays an archetypal episode of American history – a primordial incident of patriarchal domination recorded in Harriet Jacobs's *Incidents in the Life of a Slave Girl* (1861) and in countless "tragic mulatto/a" tales. His mother was acutely aware of white men's devaluation of her and Gabriel attains male currency by dominating Esther in a like manner. It is the historical desire for and abuse of black women by white men that animates Gabriel's actions.

Moreover, John emulates his stepfather's behavior when he locates Elisha as his object of desire. John subconsciously believes that he can become Gabriel's equal by forging a spiritual bond with God ("Then he and his father would be equals, in the sight, and the sound, and the love of God" [145]). Witnessing the nascent "holy" communitas in which spiritual son Elisha washed the feet of spiritual father Gabriel, John sees Elisha's value as a potential brother/lover – Elisha the privileged "other" in his father's eyes. Elisha's symbiotic function – combination brother/lover and extension of Gabriel – is also hinted at during his and John's "wrestling match," in which we see a commingling of John's burgeoning homosexuality and his protracted battle with Gabriel:

> Usually such a battle was soon over, since Elisha was so much bigger and stronger and as a wrestler so much more skilled; but tonight John was filled with a determination not to be conquered, or at least to make the conquest dear. With all the strength that was in him he fought against Elisha, and *he was filled with a strength that was almost hatred. He kicked, pounded, twisted, pushed,* using his lack of size to confound and exasperate Elisha, whose damp fists, joined at the small of John's back, soon slipped. It was a deadlock; he could not tighten his hold, John could not break it. (52–53, emphasis added)

Undergirding John's attraction to Elisha is his unresolved conflict with Gabriel, and Elisha becomes a repository for John's festering hatred of his stepfather. This is not to say that John's love for his spiritual "big brother" is motivated purely by a desire to possess someone that Gabriel values; John finds in Elisha a powerful, masculine figure who accepts him, deformities notwithstanding. Nevertheless, on some level Gabriel's "love" and "ownership" of Elisha mediate John's own desire for the supplicant's recognition; in this way he can avail himself of the masculinity, power, and recognition which Gabriel has to this point denied him.

Thus, mediated desire evident in John's and Richard's behaviors, but especially in Gabriel's, exposes the wages of black men's sins, the mimicking of whites as models for achieving voice, audience, and communitas. Their shortcomings can be viewed as Baldwin's response to Bigger Thomas: The author illumines not the total absence of black communal traditions which he feels mars *Native Son,* but the failure of black male subjects to locate within themselves and each other the power to construct alternative modes of survival. Baldwin's focus on the paradox of communitas makes a comment like Donald Gibson's particularly vexing: "The point of view [in *Go Tell It on the Mountain*] is indeed nonracial because Baldwin's premises are such that they minimize the importance of the impingement upon the lives of his characters of social, of racial realities" (Gibson 104). On the contrary, his black men internalize "racial realities" at the expense of a spiritual black brotherhood, one that Baldwin would concretize in his paean to brotherhood, "Sonny's Blues."

Earlier, I alluded to the tripartite schema Toomer enumerates in *Cane* – thesis, antithesis, and synthesis. If John embodies thesis – the black male subject as tabula rasa who achieves a tenuous sense of communitas – and Gabriel antithesis – one who sees the value of communitas but who forfeits it in order to dominate others – then Elisha signifies synthesis. I both agree and disagree with the author's comment on "minor characters," a designation usually ascribed to Elisha: "The minor characters have a certain freedom which the major ones don't. They can make comments, they can move, yet they haven't got the same weight, or intensity" (Standley and Pratt 246). Though Baldwin does not center Elisha in the same way as he does the Grimes family, Elisha resonates with a weight and intensity that transform him into a centrifugal force.

Elisha typifies the "rituals" and "field of manners" which Baldwin felt Wright ignored. And just as Toomer conveys the indelibility and centrality of the southern past with respect to the black self, Baldwin continues in the same tradition. Like so many other native southerners who have relocated, Elisha still bears the stamp of his heritage: He had "been saved at the age of eleven in the improbable fields down south" (17). Indeed, Elisha becomes what Sherley Anne Williams deems the "light bearer," the musician who functions as Baldwin's prototypic artist and prophet.[5]

Reminiscent of Langston Hughes's moaning piano player in "The Weary Blues," Elisha embodies the roots of African-American culture – the oral and performance traditions. It is his voice to which the women attending the "Tarry service" respond: "Elisha sat again at the piano and picked up his mournful song. The women rose, Sister Price first, and then Sister McCandless, and looked around the church" (56); and "Elisha began a song: 'This may be my last time,' and they began to sing" (59). Subsequently,

> The silence in the church ended when Brother Elisha, kneeling near the piano, cried out and fell backward under the power of the Lord. Immediately two or three others cried out also, and a wind, a foretaste of that great downpouring they awaited, swept the church. With this cry, and the echoing cries, the tarry service moved from its first stage of steady murmuring, broken by moans and now and again an isolated cry, into that stage of tears and groaning, of calling aloud and singing, which was like the labor of a woman about to be delivered of her first child. (113)

Unlike Gabriel's perverted call to Esther, Elisha's voice draws others nearer, prompting them to witness and locate within his humble cry their own pain. This panoply of utterances gives birth to a vocal communitas, which flowers as a result of Elisha's healing hue and cry – thus Baldwin's gestation metaphor. Though Baldwin ostensibly roots Elisha in the black gospel tradition, this "light bearer" traverses the sacred and enters the realm of the secular; he becomes the manifestation of the black archetypal blues figure. That the prescient Ralph Ellison in *Shadow and Act* can speak of Mahalia Jackson and Bessie Smith in the same breath attests to the link between the gospel and blues traditions (Ellison 219), a nexus that emerges in *Go Tell It on the Mountain.*

Baldwin spoke of the "language barrier," the difficulty of transcribing the vernacular culture of his native Harlem for his first novel: "The English language as such was not designed to carry those spirits and patterns. I had to find a way to bend it the way a blues singer bends a note" (Standley and Pratt 162). Elisha reconciles the language/music dichotomy, for his song stimulates John's own voice in both secular and sacred terms. During the banter with Elisha which precedes their wrestling, John feels "unaccustomedly bold and lighthearted" and engages in a form of signifying with his older spiritual brother (51); the reticent John becomes a "sassy nigger" whom Elisha admonishes for "running his mouth" (51–52). When Baldwin changes the context to a more traditionally "religious" one, Elisha continues to hold a central position. John hears his voice on the threshing-floor, "[a]nd a sweetness filled John as he heard this voice" (204). The prophet Elisha stimulates John's conversion, as Praying Mother Washington declares:

> Had that Boy down there on the floor a-prophesying in *tongues*, amen, just the very *minute* before Johnny fell out a-screaming, and a-crying before the Lord. Look like the Lord was using Elisha to say: "It's time, boy, come on home." (208; emphasis in original)

John himself recognizes the power of Elisha's call:

> "It was you," he said, "wasn't it, who prayed me through?"
>
> "We was all praying, little brother," said Elisha, with a smile, "but yes, I was right over you the whole time. Look like the Lord had put you like a burden on my soul." (217)

Elisha becomes the conduit through which John finds not only his voice, but also a momentary sense of communitas. Elisha conducts John's spiritual rites of passage, functioning as the newly ordained spiritual father who "kissed John on the forehead, a holy kiss" (221).

Baldwin imbues Elisha's role with (spi)ritual implications in terms of both Gabriel's and John's quests for communitas. Houston Baker's meditations on the "rites of the black (w)hole" offer a provocative and constructive framework for evaluating Baldwin's black male subjects. The black self, perpetually "under erasure" in an obdurate white culture, undergoes a tripartite passage into selfhood and wholeness. Baker summarizes his schema,

> Phase One: The black subject separates himself from the dominant white culture.
> Phase Two: The liminal stage ushers in a black subject whose desire is renewed through a spiritual and cosmic connection to African-American culture and learns to employ the internalized images of a black blues life's desire in peculiarly Afro-American ways. He also recognizes that he can never "reintegrate" into white culture.
> Phase Three: The aggregation stage in which the initiand enters a "black expressive community" and thus achieves "wholeness." (Baker 153–154)

Though the paradigm is applicable in limited degrees, it nevertheless helps delineate the levels of communitas Baldwin's male subjects achieve. Gabriel resembles the black subject in stage one, for he does maintain a physical (if not psychological) distance from white culture. Unfortunately, he squanders the chance to move beyond this initial phase; to his detriment, he has also estranged himself spiritually from the blacks with whom he shares physical but not psychic space. His verbal assaults on John and Elizabeth (whom he also slaps), coupled with his perverted "call" to Esther, emblematize a denigration of his authentic "blues" voice. John resembles the phase two "liminal" figure whose attachment to Elisha connects him to a "black blues life." A seemingly insignificant moment which occurred in John's infancy foreshadowed his inchoate blues voice: When he heard a gramophone "on a lower floor, filling the air with the slow, high, measured wailing of the blues,"[6] little Johnny "responded by wriggling, and moving his hands in the air, and making noises, meant, she [Florence] supposed, to be taken for a song" (182). Johnny senses the power of the blues as a mode

of expression and transcendence even as a little boy. Though he only reaches the threshold of communitas by the end of the novel, he at least retains a potential for brotherhood that Gabriel has foreclosed. Finally, Elisha is the herald for the black expressive community, a veritable bluesman who articulates the pain of his fellow parishioners; through his voice others "finger the jagged grain" and find lyrical forms of expression – in spirituals and testifying. That he catalyzes John's voice and offers him the potential for wholeness attests to his centrality in the novel's "constellation" of black male subjects – more than simply a minor figure or even what Fabre calls an "intermediary" (Fabre, "Fathers and Sons," 127).

The Author as Searching Subject: The Unfinished Quest for Communitas

Another ostensibly "minor" character in *Go Tell It on the Mountain,* whose life nevertheless commands perusal, is Frank, husband of Gabriel's sister Florence. To recapitulate briefly, Florence married Frank after arriving in New York. She attempts to superimpose onto him her assimilationist, middle-class ethos (Florence even uses "bleaching cream," which recalls Bone's comments about Gabriel's use of Christ as a "kind of spiritual bleaching cream," 223), but he resists fervently; moreover, he vehemently rejects Florence's Christianity, refusing to attend church because he and the Lord "don't always get along so well" (82). But perhaps the most salient features of Frank's life are two seemingly picayune ones. First, we learn that "Frank sang the blues, and he drank too much" (81); second, "He lived for a long while with another woman, and when the war came he died in France" (82).

I extract these points about Frank to establish a context for discussing Baldwin's own difficulties in achieving communitas. A secularized version of Elisha, Frank as bluesman maintains a palpable link to a black vernacular tradition that other characters in the text have forsaken. Frank "lives" the blues life – experiencing economic exigency, maintaining a strong appetite for whiskey and sex, and believing in the endless ability of blacks to "get over" in the white man's world. Florence constantly admonishes Frank for carousing with "dirty niggers"; part of his Saturday afternoon ritual involves sharing whiskey with "some ruffian." But it is Frank who also makes trenchant comments about Florence's self hatred: "Don't know why you keep wasting all your time and *my* money on all them old skin whiteners" (90). He then entreats her to "turn out that light and I'll make you to know that black's a mighty pretty color."

Though I do not mean to suggest that Frank serves as the author's surrogate or fictional doppelgänger, I contend that Frank's unstable life serves as an apt metaphor for the author's. From an artistic standpoint, one can read Baldwin's fictive oeuvre on a continuum which ends with *Just Above My Head,* which Eleanor Traylor accurately calls "a gospel tale told in the blues mode" (Traylor 95). Frank's intrinsic "blues" life, one he attempted to express in his relationships with other black men and Florence, parallels the author's internal blues voice, one so fraught with pain and pathos that he could only express it in his last novel. Though Baker traces Baldwin's search for literary expression from *Go Tell It on the Mountain* to *If Beale Street Could Talk* (1974) and concludes that his fiction and essays ultimately "reveal[s] a quest that has brought him firmly to his feet and left him speaking in an 'engaged' Black voice" (Baker, "Embattled Craftsman," 63), I would add that the quest ultimately ends with his last novel. There are other tangible connections as well: Frank's "hard drinking" certainly mirrors Baldwin's own alcoholism, and although Baldwin did not "die" in France, that country served as a front on which he waged copious and well-documented internal and artistic battles.

Thus, I will conclude this essay expatiating on how Baldwin's own perpetual and paradoxical search for communitas is mirrored in his autobiographical novel. *Go Tell It on the Mountain* becomes a *mise-en-abyme,* a "mirror text" which can be decoded as an inscribed signifier of what I view as the writer's own frustrated attempts to achieve communitas.[7]

Baldwin biographer David Leeming recalls a letter Baldwin wrote to his brother David Baldwin about being "estranged" from white and black intellectuals (304). This liminal space, one that Gabriel, John, and Richard inhabit, represented Baldwin's own anxiety of community. But the author's expressed sense of estrangement belies his efforts to find solidarity; many, including the author himself (Standley and Pratt 202–203), have commented on his quasi-filial relationship with Wright. And though his experiences in Paris during the 1950s and 1960s did not replicate the halcyon days of the Harlem Renaissance – there was no cohesive "niggerati" akin to the one Zora Neale Hurston wrote of during the 1920s – Baldwin did experience "blues moments," ephemeral periods which signaled (comm)unity:

> Once, one evening, we managed to throw the whole, terrifying subject ["art" versus "protest"] to the winds, and Richard, Chester Himes, and myself went out and got drunk. It was a good night, perhaps the best I remember in all the time I knew Richard. For he and Chester were friends, they brought out the best in each other, and the atmosphere they created brought out the best in me. Three absolutely tense, unrelentingly egotistical, and driven people, free in Paris but far from home, with so much to be said and so little time in which to say it! (*Nobody Knows* 158)[8]

This literary expatriate triumvirate recalls Gabriel, John, Richard – all of whom experience the longing for communitas, but whose own egos and paralyzing conceptions of self preclude finding it.

Another underlying theme in *Go Tell It on the Mountain* is that of near existential loneliness. Undeniably, Baldwin experienced severe angst and depression; Leeming notes that these wrenching periods resulted in both suicide attempts and hospitalization. Caribbean author Caryl Phillips writes poignantly about his visit to Baldwin's home in St. Paul de Vence, France: "The gates remind me of prison bars. I wonder if Baldwin has been in prison, or whether this exile, his homosexuality, or his very spacious home are the different forms of imprisonment" (Phillips 59); he then declares starkly, "I had never before noticed how lonely Jimmy was" (Phillips 63). This loneliness manifested itself in sometimes intriguing and even bizarre ways, perhaps most notably in the kindred connection he saw between himself and convicted child killer Wayne Williams (Baldwin used the Atlanta child murders as the basis for his extended essay, *The Evidence of Things Not Seen* [1985]). Leeming elaborates on Baldwin's interest in Williams, which provides clues as to why he envisioned himself as a voice for a tortured and voiceless "br/other":

> From the beginning, Baldwin had also been fascinated by Williams on a purely personal level. The eighties for him were years of retrospection and introspection, and he recognized in Williams a shadowlike version of what he might have been. He saw in him a lonely, homosexual, angry man who, like himself, had been denied a father's love, and who loved more than he was loved. To Joe [a lover] he had written, "A passion suppressed . . . becomes an insupportable torment"; to love and not be loved in return was to be "driven to . . . madness." (Leeming 363)

Perhaps Baldwin saw himself as a darker version of French playwright Jean Genet, an artist who personified the conceit of gay author as literary and sexual outlaw, exemplified in his graphic writings about and firsthand experiences of the prison milieu. Richard's imprisonment and suicide thus become possible metaphors for Baldwin's own spatial and psychological estrangement.

In spite of his perpetual feelings of "estrangement" and disconnectedness, Baldwin strove to construct some semblance of family, some tangible formation of men (which occasionally included women) who shared a common physical, emotional, and psychological space. Not only did he befriend an amalgam of African-American artists – Miles Davis, Bobby Short, and Cecil Brown might be considered members of his artistic communitas – but he fashioned a Hemingwayesque male environ. Black American artist Beauford Delaney was a lifelong friend who in his old age grew "a long white beard and [became] in appearance (as in reality) the archetype of the teacher and father in James Baldwin's life" (Leeming 331). Also included in his male coterie were, over at least thirty years of his life, dancer Bernard Hassel; brother David; Delaney; and perhaps the most central figure, Lucien Happersberger.

Baldwin's biographers have written of Happersberger as the

author's one true love, although they were technically lovers only briefly in the early 1950s. Happersberger was something of a literary "midwife" for *Go Tell It on the Mountain:* He provided Baldwin the isolation of a Swiss chalet so that he could complete the novel. Though Baldwin's love for Happersberger would be largely unrequited, nevertheless the Swiss "street boy" whom Baldwin met in Paris would remain a key confidante and friend who was at Baldwin's side when he passed on in 1987. Aside from this loosely connected "family," Baldwin's relationships with other men would reflect his desire for communitas; Leeming comments on the artist's proclivity for forming relationships with men considerably younger. Speaking of one such affiliation, Leeming adduces, "Once again he [Baldwin] had placed himself in a situation in which the roles of lover and father surrogate and protector were confused" (Leeming 335). Just as Elisha represents for young Johnny a substitute for Gabriel – one who can function as spiritual father and potential lover – so did Baldwin seek spiritual sons upon whom he could bestow a love he never received from his tyrannical, Gabrielesque stepfather.

Go Tell It on the Mountain holds a central position in the African-American canon. The author deftly melds the cadences of the black church and the emotional exigencies of black Southerners in a strange land, Harlem. The text also adumbrates works which confront issues surrounding male intimacy: "Sonny's Blues" (1957), which centers artistic and blood brotherhood; *Tell Me How Long the Train's Been Gone* (1968), where a Baldwinesque artist forms an uneasy love alliance with a young revolutionary; and *Just Above My Head* (1978), which addresses the trials and tribulations of four young gospel singers seeking racial, sexual, and artistic freedom. Baldwin's last novel becomes a coda, an enigmatic closure which attests to the chimeric nature of black male communitas. The perspicacious author articulates his gospel most eloquently: "In my own mind I come full circle from *Go Tell It on the Mountain* to *Just Above My Head,* which is a question of a quarter century, really" (Standley and Pratt 191). To paraphrase the redoubtable Invisible Man, the end is truly the beginning.

NOTES

1 See Hogue's chapter "The Dominant American Literary Establishment" in his *Discourse and the Other* in which he discusses the literary climate that embraced and sanctioned Wright's naturalism as an accepted literary discourse.

2 In section five of his *Stealing the Fire,* entitled " 'Outside of Disorder, The Order Which Is Art': James Baldwin and the 'Mighty' Henry James," Porter explores the intertextual relationship between Baldwin and James.

3 Terry Eagleton's *Literary Theory* contains a useful recapitulation of Lacanian and Freudian psychoanalytic theory; he uses the phrase "gendered subject" to refer to the inability of children to recognize "distinction[s] between masculine and feminine" (Eagleton 154).

4 Porter insightfully suggests that the "ironic voice" that John hears in the last section is that of his biological father; Porter also notes that Richard is the fictional voice of Wright. See section four of *Stealing the Fire,* "The 'Bitter Nourishment' of Art: The Three Faces on James Baldwin's Mountain."

5 Though Williams focuses on "Sonny's Blues" and *Blues for Mister Charlie,* her observations about the musician's "prophetic" function could just as easily be applied to *Go Tell It on the Mountain, Another Country,* and *Just Above My Head.*

6 The description here inexorably recalls the resonant final line of Ellison's *Invisible Man:* "Who knows but that, on the lower frequencies, I speak for you?" (Ellison 568).

7 I take the term *mise-en-abyme* from Jeremy Hawthorn. In *Contemporary Literary Theory* he defines it thusly: "From the French meaning, literally, to throw into the abyss. The term is adapted from heraldry, and in its adapted form generally involves the recurring internal duplication of meanings of images of an artistic whole, such that an infinite series of images disappearing into invisibility is produced – similar to what one witnesses if one looks at one's reflection between two facing mirrors. Mieke Bal recommends *mirror-text* for literary examples of *mise-en-abyme,* as in verbal examples it is not the whole of the work which is mirrored but only a part" (Hawthorn 105).

8 For a comprehensive discussion of Baldwin's experiences in Paris, see chapter thirteen of Fabre's *From Harlem to Paris,* "James Baldwin in Paris: Love and Self-Discovery."

WORKS CITED

Baker, Houston A., Jr. *Blues, Ideology, and Afro-American Literature: A Vernacular Theory.* Chicago: University of Chicago Press, 1984.

"The Embattled Craftsman: An Essay on James Baldwin." In Fred L. Standley and Nancy V. Burt, eds., *Critical Essays on James Baldwin.* Boston: G. K. Hall, 1988, pp. 62–77.

The Journey Back: Issues in Black Literature and Criticism. Chicago: University of Chicago Press, 1980.

Bakhtin, M. M. *The Dialogic Imagination.* Ed. Michael Holquist. Trans. Caryl Emerson and Holquist. Austin: University of Texas Press, 1981.

Baldwin, James. *Go Tell It on the Mountain.* New York: Laurel, 1985.

Nobody Knows My Name. New York: Dell, 1963.

Notes of a Native Son. Boston: Beacon Press, 1983.

Bone, Robert A. *The Negro Novel in America.* Revised Edition. New Haven: Yale University Press, 1965.

Dixon, Melvin. *Ride Out the Wilderness: Geography and Identity in Afro-American Literature.* Urbana: University of Illinois Press, 1987.

Douglass, Frederick. *Narrative of the Life of Frederick Douglass, An American Slave Written by Himself.* New York: Penguin, 1986.

Eagleton, Terry. *Literary Theory: An Introduction.* Minneapolis: University of Minnesota Press, 1983.

Ellison, Ralph. *Invisible Man.* New York: Random House, 1952.

Shadow and Act. New York: Random House, 1964.

Fabre, Michel. "Fathers and Sons in James Baldwin's *Go Tell It on the Mountain.*" In Keneth Kinnamon, ed., *James Baldwin: A Collection of Critical Essays.* Englewood Cliffs, NJ: Prentice-Hall, 1974, pp. 120–138.

From Harlem to Paris: Black American Writers in France, 1840–1980. Urbana: University of Illinois Press, 1991.

Foucault, Michel. *The Archaeology of Knowledge and the Discourse on Language.* Trans. A. M. Sheridan Smith. New York: Pantheon, 1972.

"What Is an Author?" In Hazard Adams and Leroy Searle, eds., *Critical Theory Since 1965.* Tallahassee: Florida State University Press, 1986, pp. 138–148.

Gates, Henry Louis, Jr. *The Signifying Monkey: A Theory of African-American Literary Criticism.* New York: Oxford University Press, 1989.

Gibson, Donald B. *The Politics of Literary Expression: A Study of Major Black Writers.* Westport, CT: Greenwood Press, 1981.

Girard, René. *Deceit, Desire, and the Novel: Self and Other in Literary Struc-*

ture. Trans. Yvonne Freccero. Baltimore: Johns Hopkins University Press, 1965.

Harris, Trudier. *Black Women in the Fiction of James Baldwin*. Knoxville: University of Tennessee Press, 1985.

Hawthorn, Jeremy. *A Concise Glossary of Contemporary Literary Theory*. London: Edward Arnold, 1992.

Hogue, W. Lawrence. *Discourse and the Other: The Production of the Afro-American Text*. Durham: Duke University Press, 1986.

hooks, bell. *Black Looks: Race and Representation*. Boston: South End Press, 1992.

Leeming, David. *James Baldwin: A Biography*. New York: Knopf, 1994.

Middleton, Peter. *The Inward Gaze: Masculinity and Subjectivity in Modern Culture*. London: Routledge, 1992.

Petry, Ann. "The Novel as Social Criticism." In Helen Hull, ed., *The Writer's Book*. New York: Harper, 1950, pp. 32–39.

Phillips, Caryl. "Dinner at Jimmy's." In Quincy Troupe, ed., *James Baldwin: The Legacy*. New York: Simon and Schuster, 1989, pp. 59–64.

Porter, Horace A. *Stealing the Fire: The Art and Protest of James Baldwin*. Middletown, CT: Wesleyan University Press, 1989.

Standley, Fred L., and Louis H. Pratt, eds. *Conversations with James Baldwin*. Jackson: University Press of Mississippi, 1989.

Thomas, H. Nigel. *From Folklore to Fiction: A Study of Folk Heroes and Rituals in the Black American Novel*. New York: Greenwood Press, 1988.

Thorsen, Karen, director. *James Baldwin: The Price of the Ticket*. California Newsreel, 1990.

Traylor, Eleanor W. "I Hear Music in the Air: James Baldwin's *Just Above My Head*." In Quincy Troupe, ed., *James Baldwin: The Legacy*. New York: Simon and Schuster, 1989, pp. 95–106.

Williams, Sherley A. *Give Birth to Brightness: A Thematic Study in Neo-Black Literature*. New York: Dial, 1972.

Notes on Contributors

Keith Clark is Assistant Professor of English at George Mason University in Fairfax, Virginia. His articles have appeared in the *African American Review* and the *Faulkner Journal*. Currently, he is preparing a book-length study on contemporary black masculinist fiction and drama, which will include discussion of James Baldwin's works.

Trudier Harris is Augustus Baldwin Longstreet Professor of American Literature at Emory University. Among her publications are *Black Women in the Fiction of James Baldwin; Fiction and Folklore: The Novels of Toni Morrison;* and *In the African Southern Vein: Narrative Strategies in Works by Zora Neale Hurston, Gloria Naylor, and Randall Kenan.* She is currently co-editing *The Oxford Companion to African American Literature.*

Michael F. Lynch is Associate Professor of English at Kent State University's Trumbull campus. He received his M.A. from John Carroll University and his Ph.D. from Kent State University. His publications include *Creative Revolt: A Study of Wright, Ellison, and Dostoevsky* as well as articles on Gloria Naylor, Richard Wright, and James Baldwin. His current project is a book-length study of James Baldwin.

Vivian M. May is pursuing a doctoral degree in Women's Studies at Emory University in Atlanta, Georgia. She has received a fellowship from the Mellon Foundation and has published an essay in *Southern Changes* entitled "Cross Purposes: Idella Parker's *Idella,* Marjorie Rawlings' 'Perfect Maid' and Marjorie Kinnan

Rawlings' *Cross Creek.*" Her wider research interests include representations of multiple identities in Canadian and American literature, narrative subversion as a means of self-representation, and literary constructions of knowledge and subjectivity.

Horace Porter is Director of African and African-American Studies and Associate Professor of English at Stanford University. He is the author of *Stealing the Fire: The Art and Protest of James Baldwin.* He is currently writing a book on Ralph Ellison.

Bryan R. Washington is Associate Professor of English at Lafayette College in Easton, Pennsylvania. He received his M.A. and Ph.D. degrees from Harvard University. He is the author of *The Politics of Exile: Ideology in Henry James, F. Scott Fitzgerald, and James Baldwin.* His current project is a book-length study on white representations of blackness in twentieth-century popular culture.

Selected Bibliography

Abramson, Doris E. *Negro Playwrights in American Theatre, 1925–1959.* New York: Columbia University Press, 1969.

Bell, Bernard W. *The Afro-American Novel and Its Tradition.* Amherst: The University of Massachusetts Press, 1987.

Bone, Robert A. *The Negro Novel in America.* New Haven: Yale University Press, 1965.

Butterfield, Stephen. *Black Autobiography in America.* Amherst: The University of Massachusetts Press, 1974.

Campbell, Jane. *Mythic Black Fiction: The Transformation of History.* Knoxville: University of Tennessee Press, 1986.

Chametzsky, Jules, ed. *Black Writers Redefine the Struggle: A Tribute to James Baldwin.* Amherst: The University of Massachusetts Press, 1989.

Davis, Arthur P. *From the Dark Tower: Afro-American Writers, 1900–1960.* Washington, D.C.: Howard University Press, 1974.

Dixon, Melvin. *Ride Out the Wilderness: Geography and Identity in Afro-American Literature.* Urbana: University of Illinois Press, 1987.

Eckman, Fern Marja. *The Furious Passage of James Baldwin.* New York: M. Evans and Co., 1966.

Forman, Enid G. *Put Me in Print: A Story of James Baldwin.* Washington, D.C.: n.d.

Gibson, Donald. *Five Black Writers: Essays on Wright, Ellison, Baldwin, Hughes, and Leroi Jones.* New York: New York University Press, 1970.

The Politics of Literary Expression: A Study of Major Black Writers. Westport, CT: Greenwood Press, 1981.

Harris, Trudier. *Black Women in the Fiction of James Baldwin.* Knoxville: University of Tennessee Press, 1985.

Hill, Herbert, ed. *Anger and Beyond: The Negro Writer in the United States.* New York: Harper and Row, 1966.

Hubbard, Dolan. *The Sermon and the African American Literary Imagination.* Columbia: University of Missouri Press, 1994.

Kenan, Randall. *James Baldwin.* New York: Chelsea House, 1994.

Kinnamon, Keneth, ed. *James Baldwin: A Collection of Critical Essays.* Englewood Cliffs, NJ: Prentice-Hall, 1974.

Leeming, David. *James Baldwin: A Biography.* New York: Knopf, 1994.

Macebuh, Stanley. *James Baldwin: A Critical Study.* New York: Third World Press/Joseph Okpaku, 1973.

Mitchell, Loften. *Black Drama.* New York: Hawthorn Books, 1967.

Moller, Karin. *The Theme of Identity in the Essays of James Baldwin: An Interpretation.* Göteborg, Sweden: Acta Universitatis Gothoburgensis, 1975.

O'Daniel, Therman B., ed. *James Baldwin: A Critical Evaluation.* Washington, D.C.: Howard University Press, 1977.

Porter, Horace. *Stealing the Fire: The Art and Protest of James Baldwin.* Middletown, CT: Wesleyan University Press, 1989.

Pratt, Louis H. *James Baldwin.* Boston: Twayne Publishers, 1978.

Rosenblatt, Roger. *Black Fiction.* Cambridge, Mass.: Harvard University Press, 1974.

Standley, Fred L. and Nancy V. Burt. *Critical Essays on James Baldwin.* Boston: G. K. Hall, 1988.

and Lewis H. Pratt, eds. *Conversations with James Baldwin.* Jackson: University of Mississippi Press, 1989.

and Nancy V. Standley. *James Baldwin: A Reference Guide.* Boston: G. K. Hall, 1980.

Sylvander, Carolyn Wedin. *James Baldwin.* New York, Ungar, 1980.

Troupe, Quincy, ed. *James Baldwin: The Legacy.* New York: Simon & Schuster, 1989.

Washington, Bryan R. *The Politics of Exile: Ideology in Henry James, F. Scott Fitzgerald, and James Baldwin.* Boston: Northeastern University Press, 1995.

Weatherby, W. J. *Squaring Off: Mailer vs. Baldwin.* New York: Mason/Charter, 1977.

GENERAL EDITOR
Emory Elliott
University of California, Riverside

剑桥美国小说新论·3

(英文影印版)

《向苍天呼吁》新论

1. 《嘉莉妹妹》新论
2. 《兔子，跑吧！》新论
* 3. 《向苍天呼吁》新论
4. 《就说是睡着了》新论
5. 《我的安冬尼亚》新论
6. 《漂亮水手》新论
7. 《白鲸》新论
8. 《所罗门之歌》新论
9. 《慧血》新论
10. 《小镇畸人》新论
11. 《白噪音》新论
12. 《瓦尔登湖》新论
13. 《太阳照样升起》新论
14. 《喧哗与骚动》新论
15. 《了不起的盖茨比》新论
16. 《尖枞树之乡》新论
17. 《麦田里的守望者》新论
18. 《永别了，武器》新论
19. 《只争朝夕》新论
20. 《八月之光》新论
21. 《海明威短篇小说》新论
22. 《汤姆叔叔的小屋》新论
23. 《他们眼望上苍》新论
24. 《红色英勇勋章》新论
25. 《贵妇画像》新论
26. 《土生子》新论
27. 《去吧，摩西》新论
28. 《美国人》新论
29. 《最后的莫希干人》新论
30. 《豪门春秋》新论
31. 《亨利·亚当斯的教育》新论
32. 《拍卖第49号》新论
33. 《觉醒》新论

CAMBRIDGE UNIVERSITY PRESS

北京大学出版社
PEKING UNIVERSITY PRESS